Poison Ivy

This weed (above) causes an itchy
rash if you touch it. Poison ivy grows
as a vine or shrub. Try to remember
what the leaves look like, and do
not touch them or other parts of
the plant. If you do touch poison
ivy, washing your hands as soon as
possible may reduce the itching.
Your local drugstore will have
various remedies that will help.

World Book's

SCIENCE & NATURE GUIDES

BIRDS

OF THE UNITED STATES AND CANADA

World Book, Inc.
a Scott Fetzer company
Chicago

Scientific names

In this book, after the common name of an organism (life form) is given, that organism's scientific name usually appears. Scientific names are put into a special type of lettering, called italic, *which looks like this.*

The first name in a scientific name is the genus. A genus consists of very similar groups, but the members of these different groups usually cannot breed with one another. The second name given is the species. Every known organism belongs to a particular species. Members of a species can breed with one another, and the young grow up to look very much like the parents.

An animal's scientific name is the same worldwide. This helps scientists and students to know which animal is being discussed, since the animal may have many different common names. Therefore, when you see a name like *Icterus galbula,* you know that the genus is *Icterus* and the species is *galbula. Icterus galbula* is the scientific name for the Baltimore oriole (see page 10).

Birdwatcher's Code

1 **Always go birdwatching with a friend,** and always tell an adult where you are going.

2 **Observe and photograph birds** without disturbing them whenever possible.

3 **Keep a good distance** from nests and nesting colonies.

4 **Leave birds in peace.** Don't chase them or make them fly unnecessarily.

5 **Don't touch or pick up fledglings or eggs.** If you do, the parents may abandon them and they will die.

6 **Keep to existing roads, trails, and pathways** wherever possible.

7 **Keep off private property** unless you have permission to go on it.

8 **Leave all gates as you find them.**

9 **Wear long pants, a hat, and a long-sleeved shirt** in tick country.

This edition published in the United States of America by World Book, Inc., Chicago.

WORLD BOOK and the GLOBE DEVICE are registered trademarks or trademarks of World Book, Inc.

World Book, Inc.
233 North Michigan Avenue
Chicago, IL 60601 USA

For information about other World Book publications, visit our Web site **http://www.worldbook.com,** or call **1-800-WORLDBK (967-5325).** For information about sales to schools and libraries, call **1-800-975-3250 (United States); 1-800-837-5365 (Canada).**

Copyright © 2005 Chrysalis Children's Book Group, an imprint of Chrysalis Books Group Plc
The Chrysalis Building, Bramley Road, London, W10 6SP
www.chrysalis.com

Library of Congress Cataloging-in-Publication Data

Birds of the United States and Canada.
    p. cm. — (World Book's science & nature guides)
    "Edited text and captions based on Birds of North America by Frank Shaw"—T.p. verso.
    Includes bibliographical references and index.
    ISBN 0-7166-4210-7 — ISBN 0-7166-4208-5 (set)
    1. Birds—North America—Juvenile literature. 2. Birds—North America—Identification—Juvenile literature. I. Shaw, Frank. Birds of North America. II. Series.

QL681 .B627 2005
598'.097—dc22

2004043486

Edited text and captions based on *Birds of North America* by Frank Shaw. Species illustrations by Norman Arlott, Trevor Boyer, Malcolm Ellis, Robert Morton, Maurice Pledger, Christopher Rose, and David Thelwell, all of Bernard Thornton Artists, London. Habitat paintings and headbands by Antonia Phillips; identification and activities illustrations by Richard Coombes.

For World Book:
General Managing Editor: Paul A. Kobasa
Editorial: Shawn Brennan, Maureen Liebenson, Christine Sullivan
Research: Madolynn Cronk, Lynn Durbin, Cheryl Graham, Karen McCormack, Loranne Shields, Hilary Zawidowski
Librarian: Jon Fjortoft
Permissions: Janet Peterson
Graphics and Design: Sandra Dyrlund, Anne Fritzinger
Indexing: Aamir Burki, David Pofelski
Pre-press and Manufacturing: Carma Fazio, Steve Hueppchen, Jared Svoboda, Madelyn Underwood
Text Processing: Curley Hunter, Gwendolyn Johnson
Proofreading: Anne Dillon

Printed in China
1 2 3 4 5 6 7 8 9 10 09 08 07 06 05 04

Contents

Introduction To Birds . . . **4–7**
What To Look For 6–7

City Parks & Suburbs . . **8–21**
Banquets for Birds 22–23

Broadleaf Forests **24–37**
Feeding Stations 38–39

Grasslands **40–47**
Out in the Wild 48–49

Deserts **50–53**
Long-distance Flyers 54–55

Evergreen Forests **56–63**
Helping Birds in Danger . . . 64–65

**Seashores &
    Marshes** **66–69**

**Lakes, Rivers, &
    Marshes** **70–77**

Find Out More 78
Index & Additional
    Resources 79–81

Entries *like this* indicate pages featuring projects you can do!

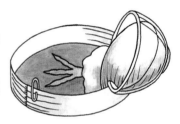

Introduction To Birds

More than 700 different types of birds breed in North America, but many other kinds—over 200 species—visit here as well. If you are not an expert birdwatcher, trying to identify one bird among so many can be hard to do.

Birds rely on their surroundings for food, places to roost (sleep), and good nesting sites, and these vary from habitat to habitat. When you know what a habitat provides, you will know what birds you might expect to see there.

This book shows only the birds you are most likely to see, and it puts them in groups according to the kind of environment where you are most likely to see them.

So, don't look for a red-throated loon in the prairies or a wood thrush by the sea. They know where they are most likely to find the food they eat. With practice, you will learn where to look for different birds.

From egg to bird

You will see birds at all stages of their lives, if you watch birds regularly. But don't expect any particular bird to look just like the picture in this book. Its color and markings may be different if it is a young bird or a female. Males are usually the more brightly colored of the two sexes. Males' markings show best during the breeding season, when they are trying to attract the females.

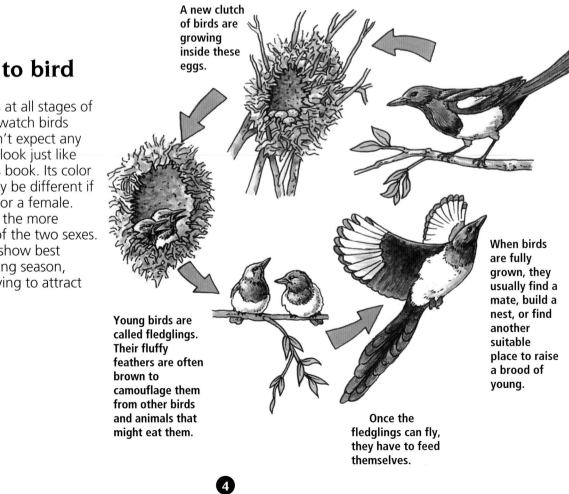

A new clutch of birds are growing inside these eggs.

When birds are fully grown, they usually find a mate, build a nest, or find another suitable place to raise a brood of young.

Young birds are called fledglings. Their fluffy feathers are often brown to camouflage them from other birds and animals that might eat them.

Once the fledglings can fly, they have to feed themselves.

How to use this book to identify birds

To identify a bird you don't recognize, follow the steps at the right.

1 **Draw a field sketch** quickly as shown on page 49. First make sure of the bird's size and shape. Then look for any special features (pages 6 to 7 show you the kinds of things you should look for).

2 **Decide what habitat you are in.** If you aren't sure, you should read the descriptions at the start of each section to see which one fits best. Each habitat has a different picture band heading. These are shown below.

3 **Look through the pages of birds** with your habitat's picture band. The picture and information given for each bird will help you identify it. The large bird (left) is a sharp-shinned hawk (see page 30).

4 **If you can't find the bird there**, look through the other sections. Birds move around and you will surely see many of them in more than one habitat. You will find the small bird (left) is a white-throated sparrow (see page 17).

5 **If you can't find the bird**, you may have to look in a larger field guide. You might have spotted a very rare bird!

Top-of-page Picture Bands

This book is divided into different habitats. Each habitat (type of environment) has a different picture band at the top of the page. These are shown below.

City Parks & Suburbs	Deserts
Broadleaf Forests	Evergreen Forests
Grasslands	Seashores & Marshes
	Lakes, Rivers, & Marshes

What To Look For

Colors and markings

When you are trying to identify a bird, look for patches of color and stripes on its wings, tail, and body. Is the color of its back different than the color of its chest or belly? Does it have eye stripes or chin stripes? Look for bands on the wings or tail. The text for each bird tells you the colors and markings you are most likely to see.

Wing bar

Crown

Forehead

Nape

Eye stripe

Back

Cheek

Chin

Flight feathers

Neck

Breast

Belly, or abdomen

Rump

Tail bar

Outer tail feathers

Bills or beaks

The shape of a bird's bill depends on the kind of food that it eats.

A sandpiper has a long, thin bill for catching insects and probing mud for food.

A heron is a wading bird. It uses its very long bill to stab fish in shallow water.

A hawk has a sharp, hooked bill for tearing meat.

A duck has a flat bill for dabbling in water to sift for plant matter.

A finch has a short, stout bill for cracking seeds.

Wing shapes

When a bird is flying, look at the shape of its wings and the pattern of its flight.

A finch has short, broad wings for flitting from tree to tree.

A swift has long, strong wings for flying for many hours.

An eagle has long, broad wings for soaring and hovering.

A gull has straight, long wings for soaring and gliding over the sea.

Feet and legs

The shapes of a bird's feet and legs are made for the way it lives.

Hawks and other birds of prey use their sharp talons for grasping their prey.

Tree-climbers, such as woodpeckers, use their long toes and claws to grip the tree trunk.

Ground birds, such as pheasants, have strong, thick toes to scratch the soil for food.

Waterbirds, such as ducks, have webbed feet for paddling through water.

City Parks & Suburbs

Pigeons, sparrows, and starlings aren't the only kinds of birds that live around the busy streets, skyscrapers, and paved areas of city centers and towns. City parks and suburbs provide food and nesting sites for many different kinds of birds. Parks provide islands of trees and grass in the sprawling concrete of cities. Suburban yards form large areas of varied shrubs and trees.

So many birds have learned to take advantage of buildings and human habitation that you may wonder how some managed before the early settlers arrived. But, of course, chimney swifts did manage without chimneys, barn swallows without buildings, and American robins without lawns.

Although the birds in this section are well adapted to living near people, you can see them in many other habitats, too. Between the suburbs and rural woodland, you often find semi-open country with scattered trees and bushes that attract several kinds of wilder birds.

If you live in an urban environment, you can encourage birds to come into your yard. The activities pages in this book will give you some ideas, but make sure that any birds that come to feed or nest are safe from cats. The picture shows nine kinds of birds from this section. How many can you identify?

Indigo bunting,
northern cardinal,
black-capped chickadee, blue jay,
American robin, chipping sparrow,
barn swallows, downy woodpecker,
house wren

Eastern & Western Screech Owls
(Otus asio)
(Otus kennicottii)

These small owls may be mainly rusty colored or gray. They have large yellow eyes and ear tufts that stand out clearly when raised. They hunt at night. Their fluffy feathers let them fly very quietly. Listen for these owls' different calls—a quavering whinny in the eastern screech owl and a series of accelerating whistles in the western screech owl. They like woods, orchards, and parks, and build their nests in tree holes or woodpecker holes. They will also use birdhouses. The females lay 4 to 6 white eggs that are incubated as soon as they are laid. Because of this, the eggs hatch at different times.

Family group: Owl
Size: 8½ in (22 cm)
Usually hunts alone
Eats insects and small animals

Baltimore Oriole
(Icterus galbula)

This bird is usually seen in the summer in suburban trees. The male is easy to see because of its black head and back, and bright orange underparts and rump. Look for the patch or stripe of white on its black wings. The female is brownish on top and deep orange below. An oriole loves to sing, so listen for its fluty whistles. Its nest is a neat pouch of grasses hung high in a tree. The female lays 4 to 6 white eggs marked with brown.

Family group: Oriole
Size: 7–8 in (18–20 cm)
Alone or in pairs
Eats insects and berries
Summer visitor

Barn Owl
(Tyto alba)

This ghostlike owl has a white breast and face and cinnamon upper parts. It hunts mainly at dawn and dusk. Although it can see very well at night, it also relies on its excellent sense of hearing to help it find its prey. Its usual call is a raspy hissing screech. It breeds in old buildings, barns, or broken trees. It nests in holes in trees or barns or in nest boxes where the female lays 3 to 8 white eggs.

Family group: Owl
Size: 15–18 in (38–45 cm)
Usually hunts alone
Eats rodents and other small creatures

Rufous Hummingbird
(Selasphorus rufus)

You will recognize this bird as a hummingbird because it hovers at flowers to sip the nectar with its long beak. You will see the rufous hummingbird only in the western parts of North America. The male rufous hummingbird has a reddish body, gray wings, and a ruby-colored throat. The female has a green back and ruby spots on her throat. She lays 2 white eggs.

Family group: Hummingbird
Size: 3–4 in (8–10 cm)
Usually feeds alone
Eats nectar of flowers
Summer visitor

Ruby-throated Hummingbird
(Archilochus colubris)

Family group: Hummingbird
Size: 3–4 in (8–10 cm)
Usually feeds alone
Eats nectar of flowers
Summer visitor

Like other hummingbirds, this bird hovers at flowers to sip the nectar with its long beak. You will see the ruby-throated hummingbird only in the eastern United States and southern Canada. The ruby-throated hummingbird is green on top and white underneath with a black tail. The male has a ruby-colored throat patch that may look black in weak light. The female lays 2 white eggs.

Blue Jay
(Cyanocitta cristata)

Family group: Jay
Size: 11–12 in (28–30 cm)
Usually alone or in pairs
Eats nuts, berries, insects, and seeds
Also found in broadleaf woods

This noisy, flashy bird is common in the eastern United States and Canada. It may be seen in the largest cities. It is easy to see with its blue upper parts and distinctive blue crest. Look for the white bands across its wings and long tail striped with black. You will easily hear its call, a loud piercing JAY-JAY. It usually makes its nest in an evergreen tree and lays 3 to 6 greenish-tan eggs spotted with brown.

Cedar Waxwing
(Bombycilla cedrorum)

Family group: Waxwing
Size: 7–8 in (18–20 cm)
Forms noisy flocks
Eats berries

There are two species of waxwings in North America. Both have sleek crests and yellow-tipped tails, but the cedar waxwing is common all over North America and is the one you are most likely to see. It roams in huge flocks along hedgerows and in yards and can quickly eat all the berries off a bush. It can even become drunk from eating fermented fruit. Waxwings nest in trees and the female lays 3 to 5 pale bluish- or purplish-gray eggs spotted with black, brown, or purple.

City Parks & Suburbs

Chimney Swift
(Chaetura pelagica)

A swift flies very fast and spends most of the day in the air. Its long, pointed wings and rounded, streamlined body are perfect for flying. It feeds, drinks, mates, gathers twigs for nests, and even washes itself while flying. The chimney swift is common in North America east of the Rockies and is the only type of swift you are likely to see there. It twitters as it flies and looks like it doesn't have a tail. It nests in chimneys, gluing its nest to the side of the chimney with saliva. The female lays 4 to 5 white eggs.

Family group:
Swift
Size: 4–5 in
(10–13 cm)
Usually in groups
Eats flying insects
Summer visitor

Northern Flicker
(Coloptes auratus)

A woodpecker is an excellent tree-climber. It has strong claws for clinging onto the bark and a sharp beak that it uses like a chisel to cut into the tree. A northern flicker uses its long, bristly tongue to catch the insects inside. The bird also likes to feed on ants on the ground. It has brown wings and back, and a white rump and underparts, all spotted with black. Its underwing may flash yellow (in the East) or orange-pink (in the West). They drill a hole in a tree or pole to make a nest where the female lays 3 to 10 white eggs.

Family group:
Woodpecker
Size: 12–13 in
(30–33 cm)
Usually alone, though they may migrate in small groups
Eats insects that dig into trees

Purple Martin
(Progne subis)

This chunky deep purple swallow has broader wings than other swallows. Look for its V-notched tail and the swallowlike way it flies—a short glide followed by rapid flapping, then another short glide. They used to nest in holes in trees or cliffs, but now often take advantage of multiple-room nest boxes that are built for them. The females lay 3 to 8 white eggs and incubate them on their own.

Family group:
Swallow
Size: 7–8 in
(18–20 cm)
Usually in large flocks
Eats flying insects
Summer visitor

Barn Swallow
(Hirundo rustica)

A swallow looks very similar to a swift and, like a swift, loves to fly. You can tell them apart because a swift flies with its wings bent closer to its body. The barn swallow is blue-black on top and rusty underneath. Look for its deeply forked tail. In the fall watch them gather in flocks on telephone wires before migrating southward. They breed over most of North America. They nest in barns and buildings and lay 3 to 8 white eggs, lightly spotted with red.

**Family group:
Swallow
Size: 6–7 in
(15–18 cm)
Usually in flocks
Eats flying insects
Summer visitor**

Downy Woodpecker
(Picoides pubescens)

This small woodpecker has a white back, striped wings, and white underparts. You can tell it apart from similar woodpeckers by its tiny beak. You are likely to see it in most of North America, clinging to the bark of a tree and boring into it in search of food. Watch for it on suburban bird feeders, too. It makes its nest by digging a hole in a dead tree. The female lays 4 to 5 white eggs.

**Family group: Woodpecker
Size: 6–7 in (15–18 cm)
Usually alone, or in pairs
Eats insects in tree bark
Also found in broadleaf or evergreen woods**

House Wren
(Troglodytes aedon)

In the spring and summer, this little brown bird is common around houses and yards all across the United States and southern Canada. Look for its chunky shape and short cocked tail. Wrens like to hide under thick plants and shrubs, but may perch in the open to sing. Listen for the house wren's loud bubbly song. It nests in a hole in a building, bird house, car, or even in a shoe or the pocket of a jacket. The female lays 6 to 8 white eggs, spotted with reddish-brown. In the fall it migrates south to the Gulf Coast and Mexico.

**Family group:
Wren
Size: 4–5 in
(10–13 cm)
Usually alone
Eats insects, spiders, and their eggs**

Common Grackle
(Quiscalus quiscula)

The male is black with pale yellow eyes. The female also has pale yellow eyes but is duller than the male. In both, look for the longish V-shaped tail. If you can get close to the male, you may notice that his head and wings have a purplish gloss. Northern and western birds may have a bronze gloss on the breast and back. They breed in trees in parks and woods. Their nests are made of twigs and grasses bound with mud. The female lays 3 to 6 pale blue or green eggs spotted with brown.

Family group: Blackbird
Size: 12–14 in (30–36 cm)
Forms large flocks
Eats insects, seeds, small animals, and berries
Also found in fields and marshes
Summer visitor in the North and West

American Crow
(Corvus brachyrhynchos)

This large, aggressive black bird is hard to miss. It lives in groups and its call is the familiar CAW-CAW. Look for its powerful beak and, if it is flying, for its square-shaped tail. It is the largest crow, and the one you are most likely to see in most parts of North America. It has adapted well to living near people. It makes its nest in a tree and builds a cup of twigs lined with any soft materials it can find. The female lays 4 or 5 greenish eggs blotched with brown.

Family group: Crow
Size: 17–21 in (43–53 cm)
Usually found in groups
Varied diet includes insects, fruits, eggs of other species
Also found in many other habitats

Gray Catbird
(Dumetella carolinensis)

This bird is slate-gray with a black cap and black tail that it often holds straight up. It is usually seen east of the Rockies. It likes to hide in dense thickets, so listen for its calls. You cannot mistake its catlike whining, and its song includes many mews, too. Its large bulky nest is made of twigs lined with grasses and roots, in which the female lays 3 to 5 greenish-blue eggs. It migrates to the Gulf and Atlantic coasts for the winter.

Family group: Thrasher
Size: 8–9 in (20–23 cm)
Usually in ones or twos
Eats insects, seeds, and berries
Also found in broadleaf woods

European Starling
(Sturnus vulgaris)

This is another aggressive bird that is hard to miss because of its shiny black plumage. The European starling was brought over from Europe in the 1890's and is now seen throughout the United States and Canada. Watch it take over at birdfeeders. In the summer its back has an iridescent green and purple sheen and its beak is yellow. In the winter it is heavily spotted all over with white and tan and its beak is dark. Listen for its twittering, particularly at dusk. Males also mimic the calls of other birds to impress females. It builds its nest in any hole it can find in a tree or building. The female lays 4 to 7 pale blue eggs there.

Family group: Starling
Size: 7½ to 8½ in (19–22 cm)
Usually in large groups
Eats insects, worms, fruit, and seeds

Northern Mockingbird
(Mimus polyglottos)

The northern mockingbird is dull gray on top, pale underneath. It has a dark gray tail and wings. Look for the white outer tail-feathers and patches of white when it is flying or preening itself. It is best known for its songs and may be heard singing from rooftops until long after dark. It will mimic other birds' songs, squeaky gates, barking dogs, and even pianos! In the spring the male may sing for hours, both day and night. The northern mockingbird nests in shrubs or low trees, and the female lays 4 to 6 bluish eggs spotted with brown.

Family group: Thrasher
Size: 9–11 in (23–28 cm)
Found alone and in pairs
Feeds on insects, seeds, and berries
Also found in woodland edges

City Parks & Suburbs

American Robin
(Turdus migratorius)

You can easily tell this well-known bird by its rich red-orange underparts and brown upper parts. Look for its streaked white bib and white lower belly. You may see it standing on the lawn with its head cocked to one side, looking for earthworms. It has a loud, melodic warble which sounds like CHEERILY, CHEER-UP, CHEERIO. Its nest is a neat cup of grasses and mud in which the female lays 3 to 5 pale blue eggs.
Family group: Thrush
Size: 9–11 in (23–28 cm)
Alone or in groups, flocking especially during migration
Eats earthworms, insects, berries

House Sparrow
(Passer domesticus)

Although this bird looks like the American sparrows, it has shorter legs and a thicker beak. Since it was brought here from Europe around 1850, it has become established wherever people live. The male is streaked black and chestnut on top and dirty gray-cream underneath. Look for his white cheeks and black bib. The female is dully colored with a streaked back. She nests in holes in buildings in cities and farms and lays three broods of 4 to 9 white eggs spotted green, brown, or black.

Family group:
Weaver finch
Size: 6–7 in
(15–18 cm)
Usually in groups
Eats seeds and
food left-overs

Chipping Sparrow
(Spizella passerina)

Sparrows are often difficult to tell apart, since they are commonly streaked brown and tan on top with pale underparts. But when it is breeding, you can tell the chipping sparrow by its chestnut crown, white stripe above its eyes, and black stripe through its eyes. Its call is a trilling CHIP-CHIP-CHIP and, in the summer, you are likely to see it feeding on lawns. It nests in trees where the female lays 3 to 4 blue eggs speckled with brown.

Family group: Sparrow
Size: 5–6 in (13–15 cm)
Usually in pairs or small groups
Eats seeds and insects
Also found in many other habitats

White-throated Sparrow
(Zonotrichia albicollis)

You are most likely to see this sparrow visiting a birdfeeder or hunched up on the ground. Look for the bold stripes on its head and for its white bib and rich chestnut upper parts. It breeds in much of Canada and the northeastern United States. It nests on the ground under a bush and lays 3 or 4 pale gray eggs, spotted with brown. In the fall you may see it migrating south, mainly to the lowlands of the eastern and southern United States, but also along the coast of California.

Family group: American sparrow and Old World bunting
Size: 6–7 in (15–18 cm)
Usually in groups
Eats insects and seeds

Northern Cardinal
(Cardinalis cardinalis)

This is one of the easiest birds to identify with its bright red crest and plumage. Look for its black face and pink beak. The female is tannish-brown with red on her wings, crest, and tail. Listen for its song—a loud ringing whistle with many variations. This is a tolerant bird that has learned to live successfully alongside people. Its nest is made of twigs and grasses. The female usually incubates the 3 or 4 grayish-white, speckled eggs spotted with brown on her own.

Family group: American bunting and grosbeak
Size: 7–9 in (18–23 cm)
Usually in pairs
Eats seeds, insects
Also found in woodland edges and marshes

Song Sparrow
(Melospiza melodia)

Most sparrows have strong feet for perching on twigs and branches, and short beaks. Watch them flit from perch to perch. Look for the song sparrow's long rounded tail, which tells it apart from other sparrows. Look at the streaking on its breast which usually leads to a central solid spot. Its song is 3 or 4 clear notes followed by a trill. It nests on the ground, building a cup of grasses in which the female lays 3 to 5 blue-green eggs spotted with brown.

Family group: Sparrow
Size: 5½–7 in (14–18 cm)
Usually in pairs or small groups
Eats seeds and insects

House Finch
(Carpodacus mexicanus)

The male is brown with a red breast and red band over his forehead and eyes. His underparts are tan streaked with brown. The female is brownish, streaked with dark brown on the top and bottom. They nest in holes in trees and buildings, in nest boxes, and in the old nests of other birds. Their 4 or 5 blue eggs are spotted with black.

Family group: Finch
Size: 5–6 in (13–15 cm)
Usually in flocks
Eats seeds, buds, and berries
Also found in dry grasslands

Common Yellowthroat
(Geothlypis trichas)

This bird is olive on top and yellow underneath. Look for the male's black face mask. It has a small beak and a rounded tail and wings. It is common and widespread, but spends much of its time living in low shrubs and plants. Listen for its song, a repeated WITCHITY. It nests on the ground all across North America. Its nest is made of stems and grass in which the female lays 3 to 5 white eggs, spotted with brown. It is a summer visitor to all but the far South and coastal states.

Family group:
Wood warbler
Size: 5–6 in
(13–15 cm)
Alone or in pairs
Eats insects
Also found in freshwater marshes

Yellow Warbler
(Dendroica petechia)

The yellow warbler is probably the most common of these small brightly colored birds. The male's yellow plumage and chestnut streaking on his breast make him easy to see, especially in the spring. In the fall he looks more like the female, paler and greener. Listen for its clear song—SWEET SWEET I'M SO SWEET. It breeds in damp thickets and builds its nest with weeds, bark, and grass, and sometimes steals material from other nests. The female lays 4 or 5 white eggs, often with a wash of green, and speckled with brown.

Family group:
Wood warbler
Size: 5–6 in
(13–15 cm)
Alone or in pairs
Eats insects
Summer visitor

Yellow-breasted Chat
(Icteria virens)

This is the largest warbler and is found over most of the United States. It is dark on top and yellow underneath. It is a shy bird and spends most of the time hiding in dense thickets and bushes. The male often sings from an open perch, or hovers with his legs dangling to impress females. Look for the small black mask and white on his face and the short chunky beak. You may hear its chattering song even at night. It makes its nest of leaves and grass where the female lays 3 to 4 white eggs spotted with brown.

Family group:
Wood warbler
Size: 7–8 in
(18–20 cm)
Usually alone
Eats insects and seeds
Summer visitor

Indigo Bunting

(Passerina cyanea)
This bunting is found only in the East. The male is blue all over, but in weak light it might look black. The female is streaked rusty-brown above, and tannish below with indistinct streaks. You may hear the male singing his warbled song long into August. The nest is a cup of leaves, bark, and grasses which the bird makes in a bush. The female lays 3 or 4 white eggs washed with blue.
Family group: American bunting and grosbeak
Size: 5–6 in (13–15 cm)—Alone or in pairs
Eats seeds, insects, and berries—Summer visitor
Also found on edges of woods and thickets

Lazuli Bunting

(Passerina amoena)

This bunting is found only in the western United States and Canada. The male is blue on top and on his neck. His breast and sides are cinnamon and his belly is white. Look for the two white bands on his wings. The female is grayish-brown with pale bands on her wings. The song is a quick series of repeated phrases. They nest in bushes. The females lay 3 to 5 white eggs washed with blue.

Family group: American bunting and grosbeak
Size: 5–6 in (13–15 cm)
Alone or in groups—Eats seeds
Also found in woods and dense growth of shrubs or trees
Summer visitor to the western U.S.

Rock Dove

(Columba livia)
These birds are also known as feral pigeons or city pigeons. They vary in color and markings, but are easy to recognize from their plump bodies and small heads. You will also recognize their familiar OO-ROO-COO call. Some pigeons are kept for racing because of their great "homing" instinct, and they were used in wartime to carry messages, even during World War II. They feed during the day in parks and fields. At night they roost on high window ledges, bridges, and barns. Most nest in trees and the females lay 2 pure white eggs. In the wild, rock doves nest on cliffs.

Family group: Pigeon
Size: 10–15 in (25–38 cm)
Usually in flocks
Eats grains, seeds, and fruit

Mourning Dove

(Zenaida macroura)

This trim-shaped pigeon has brown upper parts spotted with black and a rich pinkish breast. When it is flying it looks dark all over, so look then for its long tail tapering to a point. Listen for its call—a mournful OOOH-OO-OO-OO—and the fluttering whistle its wings make as it takes off. Its nest is a platform of twigs built in a tree in which the female lays 2 white eggs. It has a very long breeding season and usually has 5 or 6 broods each year.

Family group: Pigeon
Size: 11–12 in (28–30 cm)
Often in flocks
Eats grains, seeds, and fruit
Also found on farms and fields

Family group:
Chickadee and
titmouse
Size: 4–6 in
(10–15 cm)
Often flock
together,
especially in the
winter
Eats insects, seeds,
and berries
Also found in
broadleaf and
evergreen woods

Black-capped Chickadee
(Poecile atricapilla)

This small gray bird is easy to spot because of its black cap and bib and white cheeks. You may see it searching for food among the leaves and bark of trees or, if you put out a birdfeeder, you will probably find it is the first to arrive. Listen for it calling CHICK-A-DEE-DEE-DEE. You may see it in most of the northern United States and Canada. It makes its nest in a hole in a rotten tree stump and lays 6 to 8 white eggs, spotted with reddish-brown.

Family group:
Chickadee and
titmouse
Size: 4–6
(10–15 cm)
Often flock
together
Eats insects, seeds,
and berries

Tufted Titmouse
(Baeolophus bicolor)

This titmouse is gray on top and white underneath with a wash of warm brownish-red on its sides. Look for the dark gray crest and black forehead. This bird is common in the eastern United States although there are some in southern Texas that have black crests. You will find them eager to eat from birdfeeders. Listen for its song, a repeated PEETA, PEETA, PEETA. The female lays 5 or 6 white eggs, lightly speckled with brown.

Juniper Titmouse
(Baeolophus ridgwayi)

Titmice have short beaks, short wings, and small crests. You may see them hanging upside down from twigs while they eat. The juniper titmouse is gray on top and pale gray underneath with no other field marks to look for. Its call is a harsh SIC-A-DEE-DEE. You may see it only in the Southwest from California to Colorado. It makes its nest in a hole in a tree, building, or post, and lays 5 to 8 white eggs, lightly spotted with brown.

Family group: Chickadee and titmouse
Size: 4–6 in (10–15 cm)
Often flock together
Eats insects, seeds, and berries
Also found in woods

Eastern Phoebe
(Sayornis phoebe)

Tyrant flycatchers are often difficult to tell apart. This one is brown on top and white underneath, although in the fall its belly looks yellowish. You can recognize it best from its song—a harsh FEE-BE. Look for it perched on a branch and fluffing its feathers and spreading its tail. Wait for it to dart out after flying insects. It breeds in much of North America except on the West Coast. It often nests under bridges and lays 3 to 6 white eggs, sometimes spotted. It migrates to the Gulf and Atlantic coasts for the winter.

Family group: Tyrant flycatcher
Size: 6–7 in (15–18 cm)
Alone or in pairs
Eats flying insects
Also found in woods and on farms

Carolina Chickadee
(Poecile carolinensis)

This bird looks a lot like the black-capped chickadee (opposite page), but it is smaller and found mostly in the southeastern United States. In some places, like the Appalachians, you may see both birds but the black-capped usually keeps to higher ground. To tell them apart, listen for their songs. The Carolina chickadee's is a high-pitched fast FEE-BEE or FEE-BEE-EE. Its CHICKA-DEE call is faster. Like the black-capped, they nest in holes in dead trees and lay 5 to 8 white eggs, speckled with reddish-brown.

Family group: Chickadee and titmouse
Size: 4–5 in (10–13 cm)
Often flock together
Eats insects, seeds, and berries
Also found in broadleaf and evergreen woods

Family group: American sparrow and Old World bunting
Size: 6–7 in (15–18 cm)
Usually in small groups
Eats seeds
Also found in woods

Dark-eyed Junco
(Junco hyemalis)

You are sure to see this bird at some time of the year all over North America. It is a common visitor to birdfeeders. Look for it in the spring in the far North and in the winter in the South. It is usually gray or brown on top and on the chest with a white belly, but some birds vary in color on their head, back, and belly. Look for the white on each side of its tail when it is flying. The female lays 3 to 5 bluish-white eggs spotted with brown.

Banquets for Birds

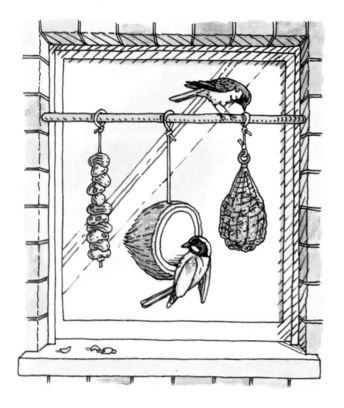

Different birds like to feed in different ways. Some like to feed on the ground, so all you have to do for these birds is to scatter some food in your yard. Others, such as warblers, feed on the seeds of trees and bushes. These birds are most likely to visit your garden if you hang pine cones and other food from your feeder. Here are some ideas for feeding these types of birds.

If you live in an apartment and do not have a yard, you still can make a small feeding station by fixing a strong pole across a window and hanging food from it. There are plenty of birds even in the busiest cities, and they soon will get used to you watching them if you keep very still.

Seeds

You can buy wild bird seed or "chick scratch" from your supermarket or pet store, but check that it contains grit. Other seeds that birds like include sunflower, millet and hemp seeds, and corn.

Don't feed the birdseed sold for cage birds to wild birds because it does not contain the right mixture of seeds.

Coconuts

Ask an adult to help you drill through one of the eyes of a coconut and drain off the milk. Then ask the adult to saw a section off the side about an inch away from the drilled eyehole (about a quarter of its length). Drill another hole through the second eye and thread some wire or plastic string through the holes, so that you can hang the coconut from a branch or the edge of a feeding station.

Scraps

Bacon rinds, fruit like apple cores or orange segments, shelled unsalted peanuts, and water-soaked raisins are all good food for birds. **Beware** of feeding too many cake or breadcrumbs, because these fill the bird's stomach without giving it the energy it needs.

Peanut chains

Buy some raw peanuts in their shells. Get some thin wire and string the peanuts on it by pushing the wire through the middle of the shell. Secure with a knot below bottom peanut. Put about 10 to 12 nuts on each wire and hang them up from a branch or the edge of a feeding station.

Alternatively you can tie the peanuts into a row with a string around their middles. These nuts may also attract squirrels.

Pine cone feeders

1 **Collect seven or eight pine cones** (the short, squat sort work best).

2 **Ask an adult to melt 2 ounces (57 grams) of lard** in a pan and set it aside to cool.
3 **Stir in 1 ounce (28 grams) of all-natural peanut butter** plus a large tablespoon of flour or cornmeal. (The flour or meal is important because it soaks up the grease from the peanut butter).

4 **When the mixture is cool, but still runny**, roll the pine cones in it until all the crannies are filled.
5 **Screw an eye-screw into the stem** of each pine cone, and then use a wire or some string to hang them up from a branch or the edge of a feeding station. These pine cones can be refilled when the birds have eaten the lard.

Suet cake

1 **Melt 2 ounces of lard** in a pan. Ask an adult to help.
2 **Stir in 2 ounces of wild birdseed,** which you can buy in a market or pet store.

3 **Pour the mixture very carefully** into a plastic yogurt or cottage cheese container, large enough to hold it.

4 **Push the end of a piece of string** down through the middle of the mixture with a skewer. Leave the cake to cool and harden before you remove the container.
5 **Tie the cake to the branch of a tree** or the edge of a feeding station.

Broadleaf Forests

Here you will see plenty of oaks, maples, hickories, willows, beeches, elms, cottonwoods, and locusts. These trees have broad leaves and lose them in the fall. Overhead they meet to form a thick, high canopy, while small shrubs and plants grow in the deep shade on the forest floor underneath.

Many kinds of birds live here—woodpeckers, woodland hawks, thrushes, and warblers. The trees and shrubs provide a varied diet of seeds and insects and, of course, many places for the birds to roost and nest. You will have to be patient to see forest birds. Many are shy and keep themselves hidden in the leaves and shrubs. But you will definitely hear them. Learning to recognize their songs will help you to identify them.

Spring and summer are the best times to look for birds in these forests. About three-quarters of the birds that breed here migrate south for the winter. Look for some of the birds from evergreen forests (shown between pages 56 and 63) too, as they also come to broadleaf and mixed woods.

Where forests have been cleared, thickets—small trees, bushes, and shrubs—might grow in their place. Look out for warblers, sparrows, and finches in thickets and on the edge of forests. Many of these birds winter here. The picture shows 10 kinds of birds from this section. How many can you identify?

Yellow-billed cuckoo, rose-breasted grosbeak, great horned owl, scarlet tanager, wood thrush, wild turkey, turkey vulture, black-and-white warbler, hairy woodpecker, redheaded woodpecker

Wild Turkey
(Meleagris galloparo)

**Family group:
Game bird
Size: male 46 in
(117 cm);
female 37 in
(94 cm)
Forages in groups
Eats seeds, nuts,
acorns, insects
Also found in
scrub**

You cannot mistake this large game bird. Its body and wings are deep bronze-colored with white stripes. Look for the red wattles along the neck. The male has a large tail, which it opens like a fan to attract the female. It spends most of its time foraging on the ground although it roosts in trees at night. In spring the male gobbles so loudly it can be heard up to a mile (or kilometer) away. Females are smaller and less colorful than males. The eggs are tan, speckled with reddish-brown, and the female lays 8 to 15 on the ground, hidden under thick undergrowth.

Ruffed Grouse
(Bonasa umbellus)

**Family group:
Grouse
Size: 16–17 in
(41–43 cm)
Usually alone
Eats seeds, insects,
berries, and plant
buds
Also found in
mixed woodlands**

This bird goes through two color phases—red and gray. The change is most noticeable in its large tail with bands of either red or gray across it. Look for the wide dark band near the tip. Look for the small crest on its head, too. You are most likely to see a ruffed grouse in a brushy forest. When it is disturbed, it bursts into flight with a roar of wings. In the spring the male tries to attract the female by beating his wings making a drumming sound. The eggs are tan and lightly speckled brown and 9 to 12 are laid in May or June in a hollow next to a tree or rock.

Great Horned Owl
(*Bubo virginianus*)

This owl is big and powerful with large rounded wings. It has long ear tufts like the long-eared owl, but you can easily tell them apart by the great horned owl's enormous size and white throat. It hunts at night and its call is a deep HOOO-HOO-HOO. Its eggs are white and the female lays 2 or 3 of them between January and April. It may use an unused nest or make its own in trees, caves, or on a sheltered place on the ground.

Family group: Owl
Size: 24 in (61 cm)—Hunts alone
Eats small and large prey, including skunks and grouse
Also found in other habitats

Barred Owl
(*Strix varia*)

This medium-sized owl has dark rings around its eyes and face, wide stripes across its upper breast, and dark streaking down its belly. It likes damp woodlands and hunts mainly at night, when you might hear it clearly hooting OO-OO-OOO-OOOO. During the day, it is well hidden on its roost, but, since it is easily disturbed, you may hear it hooting then, too. The eggs are white and the female lays 2 or 3 between February and April, usually in a hole in a tree or in an unused nest.

Family group: Owl
Size: 20–22 in (51–56 cm)
Hunts alone
Eats rodents, birds, and small animals
Also found in evergreen forests

Yellow-billed & Black-billed Cuckoos
(*Coccyzus americanus*)
(*Coccyzus erythropthalmus*)

Cuckoos have slim bodies and long tails with black-and-white bands underneath. The yellow-billed and black-billed cuckoos are both brown on top and white underneath. The color of their bills, and the white tail spots of the yellow-billed, are the best way to tell them apart. The yellow-billed is common all over the United States except in the northwestern states and California. Look for the cinnamon color in its wings as it flies. Its song is a hollow but sharp KUK-KUK-KUK. She builds a nest of twigs, but sometimes she lays her 3 or 4 greenish-blue eggs in the nest of another bird.

Family group: Cuckoo
Size: 10–12 in (25–30 cm)
Usually alone
Feeds mainly on caterpillars and other insects
Summer visitor

Redheaded Woodpecker
(Melanerpes erythrocephalus)

The redheaded woodpecker is black on top and white underneath, and its whole head and throat are red. Look for the white patch on its wings and its white rump. It is found east of the Rocky Mountains in the United States and Canada. You will probably hear it before you see it, drilling with its sharp beak into the bark of a tree. But you could also see it on the ground searching for food. The female lays 4 to 7 white eggs in a hole dug out of a dead tree or dead limb.

Family group: Woodpecker
Size: 9–10 in (23–25 cm)
Usually alone
Eats insects, nuts, and berries
Also found in parks and gardens

Pileated Woodpecker
(Dryocopus pileatus)

This large, black woodpecker has a red crest and white lines on its face. When it is flying look for the white under its wings. Look for the large, rectangular or oval nest holes it excavates in trees, too. Like all woodpeckers, it likes to make a new nest hole every year, and so provides a constant supply of old nest holes for other kinds of birds to use. It lives in the eastern United States and across central and southern Canada to the West Coast. The female lays 3 to 5 white eggs.

Family group: Woodpecker
Size: 15–17 in (38–43 cm)
Usually alone
Eats ants and other insects in trees and stumps
Also found in parks

Yellow-bellied Sapsucker
(Sphyrapicus varius)

As its name suggests, you can tell this bird by its yellow underparts. Look for the red forehead, white wing patch, and white rump. The male has a red chin and throat. Sapsuckers drill holes in the trunk of a tree, then return later to feed on the sap and insects that have gathered in the holes. This bird breeds in forests in Canada and the northeastern United States. The female lays 3 to 7 white eggs in a hole dug into a dead or dying tree. In the fall, the bird migrates to the Southern States and Mexico.

Hairy Woodpecker
(Picoides villosus)

You may see this woodpecker in forests all the way across North America. Look for its white back and the white stripes on its wings. Its face is black and white with red on the back of its head. It looks similar to the downy woodpecker but has a larger bill. Like all woodpeckers, it has short legs and claws to give it a good grip when climbing, and it uses its stiff tail feathers to support itself as it cuts into a tree. The female lays 3 to 6 white eggs in a hole dug into a tree.

Family group: Woodpecker
Size: 9–10 in (23–25 cm)
Usually alone
Eats insects that bore into tree bark

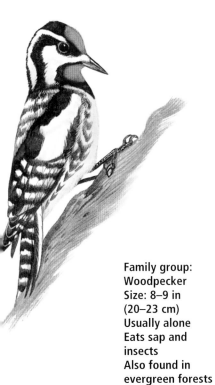

Family group: Woodpecker
Size: 8–9 in (20–23 cm)
Usually alone
Eats sap and insects
Also found in evergreen forests
Summer visitor

Acorn Woodpecker
(Melanerpes formicivorus)

You may see this noisy, sociable woodpecker in California and parts of the southern United States. It is shiny black on top, white underneath with a broad black breast and streaked belly. Look for its red cap. Listen for its call—a nasal WAKA. It has the unusual habit of drilling small holes in trees or poles and storing acorns in them for the winter. The female lays 3 to 7 white eggs and, unlike other woodpeckers reuses its previous nest.

Family group: Woodpecker
Size: 9–10 in (23–25 cm)
Usually in small noisy groups
Eats acorns and nuts in winter, insects in summer

Broadleaf Forests

Cooper's Hawk
(Accipiter cooperii)

You may see this hawk throughout the year in the United States and southern Canada. It looks like the sharp-shinned hawk except that it is larger and its long tail is rounded at the end, not squared. Watch it soar with fast wing-beats interrupted by periods of gliding. The female lays 3 to 5 off-white eggs.

Family group: Hawk
Size: 14–19 in (36–48 cm)—Usually alone
Preys on songbirds and small mammals

Broad-winged Hawk
(Buteo platypterus)

This hawk perches on a low branch waiting for its prey. It is brown on top with white underparts banded with rust. Look for its hooked bill and sharp talons. If it is flying, you will easily see its broad white wings edged with black and its black-and-white banded tail. It breeds in the eastern United States up to the Gulf of St. Lawrence. Its call is a high-pitched whistle. It will often use the old nest of a crow or make its own nest. The female lays 2 to 4 whitish eggs spotted with brown.

Family group: Hawk
Size: 16 in (41 cm)
Migrate in flocks, spending winter in South America
Preys on mice, snakes, and small birds

Sharp-shinned Hawk
(Accipiter striatus)

This hawk is gray above and chestnut below with white stripes. When it is flying, look for its long squared tail with four or five clear dark bands and for its rounded wings. Its call is a high-pitched KEE-KEE-KEE. It breeds in Canada and parts of the northern United States. Its nest is a large well-built cup of twigs, usually hidden high in an evergreen tree. The female lays 3 to 6 white eggs with brown spots. In the fall it migrates south to Panama.

Family group: Hawk
Size: 9–13 in
(23–33 cm)
Usually alone but may migrate in loose groups
Preys on small birds, some insects, and rodents
Also found in mixed woodlands

Whippoorwill
(Caprimulgus vociferus)

This bird is hard to spot but easy to hear. Its clear WHIP-POOR-WILL call gives it its name. Its overall gray-brown color camouflages it well, but look for its long rounded tail and black chin with a white "necklace." It feeds after dark, catching moths and insects as it flies. It breeds in eastern states and the Southwest. The female lays 2 white eggs spotted with gray. In the fall it migrates to the Gulf Coast and Florida.

Family group: Nightjar
Size 9–10 in (23–25 cm)—Feeds alone
Eats flying insects
Also found in evergreen forests

Red-shouldered Hawk
(Buteo lineatus)

You may see this hawk in most woodlands in eastern states and California. It is one of the easiest to see during the day. When it is soaring high in the sky, look for its large, rounded wings with clear black-and-white bands on its flight feathers, and its dark gray tail with narrow white bands. Its call is a high-pitched KEE-AH or KAH. It nests high in a tree and lays 2 to 4 white eggs spotted with brown.

Family group: Hawk
Size: 17 in (43 cm)
Usually alone or in small flocks in fall
Preys on snakes, frogs, mice, crayfish, young birds

Turkey Vulture
(Cathartes aura)

You can tell this vulture by its bald, red head and large, hooked bill. Its talons are too weak to grab live prey, so it feeds instead on carrion and garbage. It soars and glides on its large wings which it holds in a shallow V. Look for the flight feathers, which are clearly paler than the rest of the wing and the body. It breeds in the United States and southern Canada. It does not make a nest, but simply lays its 2 pale yellow eggs, blotched with brown, on bare ground or cliffs.

Family group: Vulture
Size: 26 in (66 cm)—Often soars in loose groups
Scavenges on garbage dumps and on dead animals
Also found in many other habitats

Broadleaf Forests

Eastern & Western Wood-pewees

(Contopus virens)

(Contopus sordidulus)

There are two kinds of wood-pewees that nest in North America. It's hard to tell them apart but this doesn't matter because their ranges don't overlap. Both are dull brown on top with two white bars on the wings, and whitish underneath. Listen for the PEE-A-WEE call of the Eastern bird and the PEE-ER call of the Western bird. Both birds make their nest on a horizontal tree branch and lay 2 to 4 white eggs, spotted with brown.

Family group: Flycatcher
Size: 6–8 in (15–20 cm)—Alone or in pairs
Eats flying insects—Summer visitor

Bewick's Wren

(Thryomanes bewickii)
Wrens are small, chunky birds with long, curved bills. They are very active and curious. They can often be tempted into the open by squeaky noises. The Bewick's wren holds its long tail high above its back and wags it from side to side. It has a brown back and white underparts. Look for the white stripe over its eyes. It is more common in the western United States than the East. It makes its nest in old woodpecker holes, nest boxes, and other holes. The 5 to 7 white eggs are spotted with brown.

Family group: Wren
Size: 4–5 in (10–13 cm)—Usually alone—Eats insects

Brown Creeper

(Certhia americana)

You might find this bird in most parts of North America in winter. You will probably hear its high-pitched SEE-SEE-SEE call before you see it. It is brown-and-tan streaked on top with white underparts. Look for it on a tree trunk, digging its long, curved bill into the bark to search out insects and larvae. It breeds in southern Canada. It usually builds its nest beneath a piece of loose bark. The female lays 5 to 8 white eggs speckled with reddish-brown.

Family group: Creeper—Size: 5–6 in (13–15 cm)
Usually alone, but may join flocks of titmice and nuthatches in winter
Eats insects and larvae from bark

Fox Sparrow

(Passerella iliaca)

Family group: Sparrow
Size: 7 in (18 cm)
Usually in small groups
Eats mainly seeds

This sparrow varies in the color of its plumage, but always has white underparts with spots or streaks. It usually has a rust-colored rump and tail and many have a two-toned bill. Watch it kick both feet backward as it feeds in leaf trash. It breeds in northern Canada and Alaska and southward through the Rockies. It nests on the ground under a bush where the female lays 4 or 5 white eggs washed blue or green and spotted with brown. In the winter, you may see it on the Pacific coast and in the Southern States.

Wood Thrush
(Hylocichla mustelina)

You will see this chubby bird only in the eastern United States. It is the largest of the brown and spotted thrushes. Look for its reddish-brown back (especially around the head) and large dark breast spots. It sings loudly and tunefully in phrases of 3 to 5 notes. It makes its nest of grass and mud and lines it with roots. The 3 to 5 greenish-blue eggs are incubated by the female alone.

Family group: Thrush
Size: 7–8 in (18–20 cm)
Alone or in groups
Eats insects and berries
Summer visitor
Also found in swamps and suburbs

Ovenbird
(Seiurus aurocapillus)

You are most likely to see this bird foraging for food on the ground. It is olive-brown above and white streaked with black underneath. Try to spot the reddish crown bordered by black stripes. Look, too, for its pink legs. It walks, rather than hops, with its tail cocked. It is common in the Eastern States and much of Canada. Its song is a loud TEACHER-TEACHER-TEACHER. It makes an ovenlike nest among fallen leaves on the ground and lays 4 to 6 white eggs speckled with brown.

Family group: Wood warbler
Size: 5–6 in (13–15 cm)
Usually alone
Eats insects and tiny ground animals
Summer visitor, though a few spend the winter in Florida

Veery
(Catharus fuscescens)

This bird is a typical small thrush, but you can tell it apart from others by its blurry breast spots and uniform, reddish-brown coloring on top. Like other thrushes it is white underneath with a speckled breast. It is named after its song—a series of descending VEER notes. It is a common but shy bird. Look for it in damp woodlands and thickets along the United States-Canada border and in the Appalachians and Rockies. It builds its nest on the ground using twigs and grass and lays 3 to 5 greenish-blue eggs.

Family group: Thrush
Size: 7 in (18 cm)
Alone or in groups
Eats insects and berries
Summer visitor

Orchard Oriole

(Icterus spurius)

Orioles have long tails and pointed beaks. The male orchard oriole has a chestnut body and black hood, wings, and tail. Instead of chestnut, the female is greenish on top and greenish-yellow underneath. You are most likely to see them in the eastern United States in orchards or other areas of scattered trees. Its nest is a hammock of grasses hung from a fork in a tree, and the female lays 3 to 7 white eggs spotted with brown. Sometimes more than one pair of birds may nest in the same tree.

Family group: Blackbird
Size: 7–8 in (18–20 cm)
Usually alone or in pairs
Eats insects and berries
Also found in suburbs
Summer visitor

Black-headed Grosbeak

(Pheucticus melanocephalus)
This large finch has a heavy, triangular bill. The male has a black head, black back, black tail, and black-and-white wings. Look for his rich cinnamon-colored underparts. The female is brown on top with a tan, slightly streaked breast. You are most likely to see it in the western United States along the edges of woodlands and in clearings. Its nest is a platform of twigs in which the female lays 2 to 5 greenish-blue eggs spotted with brown. The male has the unusual habit of singing while taking his turn to sit on the eggs.

Family group: American bunting and grosbeak
Size: 8–9 in (20–23 cm)
Usually alone
Eats seeds, berries, and insects
Summer visitor

Family group: Bunting and sparrow
Size: 8–9 in (20–23 cm)
Usually alone or in small groups
Feeds on insects and seeds on the ground

Eastern Towhee

(Pipilo erythrophthalmus)

Eastern towhees have long tails, white underparts, and chestnut sides. The male is black on top and the female is brown. Look for the white outer tail feathers and patch of white on the wings. You might see it in most of the United States and southern Canada at some time of the year. Watch it scratching the ground for food with both feet together. Listen for its call. In the West it is TOW-WEE and in the East DRINK-YOUR-TEA. The female lays 2 to 6 white eggs spotted with brown.

American Redstart
(Setophaga ruticilla)

This bird is easy to spot by the colorful patches on its wings and tail. The male is black with a white belly and orange-red patches. The female is brown or olive-green with patches of yellow where the male is orange. Look for it chasing flying insects, or watch it as it perches, spreading its wings and fanning out its tail (done by males only during courtship). It breeds in most of North America except for the far North and the Southwest. It nests in a tree and lays 4 or 5 white eggs speckled with brown.

Family group: Warbler
Size: 5–6 in (13–15 cm)
Alone or in small groups
Eats flying and other insects
Summer visitor, though a few spend the winter in southern Florida

Rose-breasted Grosbeak
(Pheucticus ludovicianus)

This chunky bird is black on top, white underneath, and has a red breast. The female is brown on top and tan streaked with brown underneath. Look for the thick white bill. You are most likely to find this bird in the northeastern United States and Canada, but also farther west in Canada. It likes re-growing or open woodlands. Its nest is a platform of twigs placed high in a tree in which the female lays 3 to 5 green-blue eggs speckled with brown.

Family group: American bunting and grosbeak
Size: 8–9 in (20–23 cm)
Usually alone
Eats seeds, berries, and insects
Summer visitor

Scarlet Tanager
(Piranga olivacea)

The male is one of the most beautiful birds of North American woodlands. Only the black wings and tail break up the brilliant scarlet. The female is greenish-olive on top and yellowish underneath. You might hear its harsh whistling in the summer in woods in the Eastern States. Its nest is a loose cup of twigs and grasses built high up on the end of a tree branch. The female lays 3 to 5 blue-green eggs spotted with brown. It migrates to South America for the winter.

Family group: Tanager
Size: 7–8 in (18–20 cm)
Alone or in pairs
Eats insects and berries
Summer visitor

Broadleaf Forests

Prairie Warbler
(Dendroica discolor)

Like many warblers, this bird is olive-green on top and yellow underneath. Look for the black streaks on its sides and the patch of yellow surrounded by black under its eyes. In the spring and summer you may see it in thickets in the eastern United States and southeastern Canada. Look for it twitching its tail as it forages in low shrubs and brush. Despite its name, it is not a prairie bird. It nests in low bushes and the female lays 3 to 5 white eggs speckled with brown.

Family group:
Wood warbler
Size: 4–5 in
(10–13 cm)
Usually alone
Eats insects
Summer visitor,
though a few
spend the winter
in southern Florida

Nashville Warbler

Family group:
Wood warbler
Size: 4–5 in
(10–13 cm)
Usually alone
Eats insects
Summer visitor

(Vermivora ruficapilla)
You will easily spot this bird's yellow underparts. Look for the gray head and the white ring around its eyes, too. You are most likely to see it in re-growing woods and in damp spruce bogs. Listen for its SEE-WEET song. It breeds along the Canada-United States border, but not in the prairies. It nests on the ground and lays 4 to 6 white eggs spotted with reddish-brown.

Hooded Warbler
(Wilsonia citrina)

The male has a very clear black hood and yellow face. The female is yellow underneath and green on top, like the male, but has only faint black markings. This bird likes to hide in damp woodlands so you are more likely to hear it than see it. Its song is a loud, musical whistle that sounds like TA-WIT TA-WIT TA-WIT TEE-YO. It breeds in the eastern United States and builds a bulky nest of leaves and grasses. The female lays 2 to 7 white eggs spotted with brown.

Family group:
Wood warbler
Size: 5–6 in
(13–15 cm)
Usually alone
Eats insects and
spiders
Summer visitor

Wilson's Warbler
(Wilsonia pusilla)

Family group:
Wood warbler
Size: 4–5 in
(10–13 cm)
Usually alone
Eats insects, often
while flying
Summer visitor

This warbler was named after Alexander Wilson, a famous Scottish-American birdwatcher. It looks like the hooded warbler except that the male has black only on the crown of his head. The female has no black. Listen for its song—a long descending series of CHIP notes. It breeds in damp thickets in northern Canada and much of the West. It makes a large nest of leaves and grasses, well hidden, on the ground. The female lays 4 to 6 white eggs speckled with brown.

Red-eyed Vireo
(Vireo olivaceus)

This bird is common in the eastern United States and Canada. It is olive-brown on top and white underneath. Look for the black-and-white stripes over its eyes. Its red eyes are difficult to see unless you are lucky enough to get very close to it. You will certainly hear it, though, because it sings all day during the spring and summer as it searches through the bushes for food. The female lays 2 to 4 white eggs spotted with reddish-brown. They migrate to tropical forests in South America for the winter.

Family group: Vireo
Size: 6 in (15 cm)—Usually alone or in small groups
Eats insects in the summer, berries in the fall and winter
Summer visitor

White-eyed Vireo
(Vireo griseus)

Although this bird is common in the eastern United States, you'd be lucky to get a good look at it because it likes to hide in dense thickets. It sings loudly, a scolding five- to seven-note song, beginning and ending with a sharp CHIP. If you see it, look for the two whitish wing bars on its olive-green wings. Try to get close enough to see its yellow "eye glasses" and white eyes. It lines its nest with lichens and spiders' webs and the female lays 3 to 5 white eggs spotted with brown.

Family group: Vireo
Size: 4–5 in (10–13 cm)
Usually alone
Feeds mostly on insects and berries

Family group: Wood warbler
Size: 5–6 in (13–15 cm)
Alone or in loose groups
Eats insects
Summer visitor

Black-and-white Warbler
(Mniotilta varia)

Both males and females are boldly marked with black and white. Look particularly for the black-and-white stripes on the crown. Watch for them climbing up and down tree trunks and branches, like creepers do, looking for insects to eat. Listen for its song, a series of high, thin WEE-WEE notes. It breeds in the Eastern States, stretching farther north and west in Canada. It hides its nest among the roots of a tree where the female lays 4 to 6 white eggs spotted with reddish-brown.

Feeding Stations

The best place to start bird watching is in your own yard. And the best way to attract birds there is to put out food and water for them. You will have no trouble enticing pigeons, starlings, and other common birds to come and feed. In fact, you probably will be surprised by how many different kinds you see. However, you are more likely to get some of the smaller seed-eating birds like finches and chickadees if you make a feeding station.

Simple bird feeder

1 **Find an old plastic tray** and ask an adult to drill some holes around the edge. One at each corner plus two or three more along each edge will do.
2 **Loop some nylon cord** through the holes at each corner to hang it by. The others holes are to let rainwater drain off.
3 **Hang the feeder from the branch of a tree** as far out of the way of cats and squirrels as you can. Tie the cord firmly.

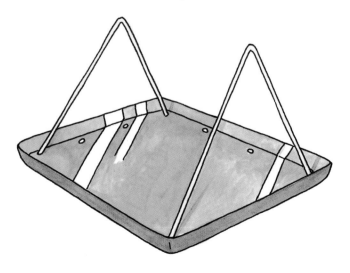

Wooden bird feeder

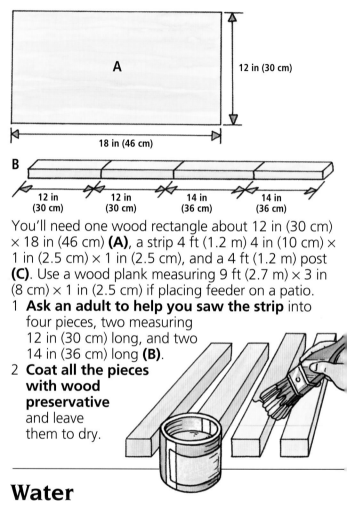

A

12 in (30 cm)

18 in (46 cm)

B

12 in (30 cm) 12 in (30 cm) 14 in (36 cm) 14 in (36 cm)

You'll need one wood rectangle about 12 in (30 cm) × 18 in (46 cm) **(A)**, a strip 4 ft (1.2 m) 4 in (10 cm) × 1 in (2.5 cm) × 1 in (2.5 cm), and a 4 ft (1.2 m) post **(C)**. Use a wood plank measuring 9 ft (2.7 m) × 3 in (8 cm) × 1 in (2.5 cm) if placing feeder on a patio.

1 **Ask an adult to help you saw the strip** into four pieces, two measuring 12 in (30 cm) long, and two 14 in (36 cm) long **(B)**.
2 **Coat all the pieces with wood preservative** and leave them to dry.

Water

Birds also need extra water when the ground is frozen. If the water freezes, replace it with fresh water.

At any time of the year, birds will enjoy a bird-bath. You can make this quite simply from the lid of a garbage can, a large potted-plant saucer, or some other wide, shallow basin. If you make sure there is always water in it, the birds will soon know where to come for a drink or a bath.

If you use the lid of a garbage can, support it with bricks or stones on four sides. Put a heap of small stones in the middle so that the water does not get too deep for small birds.

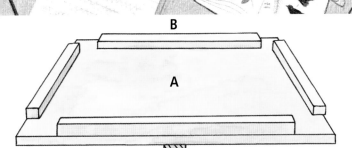

3 **Glue or nail the four strips of wood (B)** on to the rectangle **(A)** as shown. The gaps at each corner are very important because they let rainwater run off and make it easier to clean the tray.

4 **Nail the post (C)** onto the underside of the board in the center.

5 **For a patio, cut the plank into eight pieces:** four measuring 12 in (30 cm) long **(D)**, plus four pieces measuring 15 in (38 cm) **(E)** each.

6 **Nail the four 12-in (30-cm) strips (D)** to the bottom of the post to make feet. Then nail on the four 15-in (38-cm) diagonal pieces **(E),** as shown, to make the feeder stand up on its own.

Where to put the feeder?

Before you decide where the feeder is to go, think about where it will be safest from cats and squirrels. Remember that both are good jumpers. Try to keep it away from shrubs, fences, and walls.

The second thing to think about is: Can you see it from your house? You want to be able to watch the birds without disturbing them.

Looking after the feeder

Once you start putting out food for the birds, make sure you keep doing it. They will expect it! In the wintertime, when the ground is frozen and many of the trees are bare, is when the birds most need extra food. Suggestions for different kinds of food are given on pages 22-23.

Before adding new food, make sure that the tray is clean. If there are bird droppings among the leftover seeds, throw them away, too.

Use warm, soapy water to wash the tray, then rinse and dry it before adding new food.

Grasslands

This section covers a variety of habitats, but they all have one thing in common—the main type of plant growing there is grass of one kind or another. They may be prairies of natural grass, grassy pastures for grazing animals, meadows, or fields of short grass or other crops.

The grass could be tall, medium, or short—that depends on the amount of rainfall the region gets. You won't see many trees, apart from a few on a savanna, but you will see many wild flowers.

Which birds you are likely to find will vary according to the kind of grassland. Open farmland might have only a few birds, like meadowlarks, horned larks, and maybe one or two killdeers. Grassy meadows used for grazing cattle will attract more birds, but wide areas of natural grassland support many different kinds.

Write down what kind of grassland it is where you see a bird and see if you can connect it to what the bird eats and where it nests. Kingbirds, magpies, and the red-tailed hawk often feed in fields, but need trees to nest in. Bluebirds and kestrels nest in tree holes, but will use nest boxes near open fields. Meadowlarks, killdeers, and many other kinds of grassland birds, however, nest on the ground. The picture shows nine kinds of birds from this book. How many can you identify?

Eastern and western bluebirds, American crow, red-tailed hawk, killdeer, eastern kingbird, horned larks, black-billed magpie, meadowlark, ring-necked pheasants

Grasslands

Northern Harrier
(Circus cyaneus)

This bird of prey has long, narrow wings and a long tail. Look for it flying low over the ground, its wings raised up, looking for its prey. The male is gray on top and white underneath, with black tips on its wings. The female is brown above and mottled tan below. Look for the white band across the rump on both the male and the female. The harrier nests in the northern United States and Canada, and flies south for the winter. The female lays 4 to 6 eggs. The eggs are white with a wash of blue, spotted with brown.

Family group: Hawk
Size: 17–24 in (43–61 cm)
Hunts alone
Eats mice, rats, frogs, and other prey
Also found in open fields

Loggerhead Shrike

(Lanius ludovicianus)

Shrikes perch on a branch and scan the ground for prey. Then they pounce on it with their large, hooked beaks. They store their prey on thorns and barbed wire. There are two kinds of shrike in North America and they are hard to tell apart. The loggerhead shrike is slightly smaller and darker than the northern shrike, which is mainly a winter visitor. Both are gray with black wings and tail. Look for the black mask stretching across the eyes and the patch of white on the wings. The loggerhead shrike makes its nest in bushes and hedges and lays 4 to 6 gray-white eggs with brown spots.

Family group: Shrike
Size: 8–10 in (20–25 cm)—Usually hunts alone
Preys on insects, small birds, and rodents

Red-tailed Hawk
(Buteo jamaicensis)

This is one of the most common hawks. You are likely to see it over open fields near woodlands. It is brown on top and pale underneath. Look for the narrow, dark band across its belly and the plain, reddish-orange tail. Its wings are broad and roundish. You will easily see it circling high in the sky, waiting to pounce on its prey below with its hooked beak and sharp talons. Listen for its high-pitched, distinctive KEE-ARGH call. Its nest is a heavy mass of twigs built high in a tree. The female lays 2 to 4 white eggs speckled with brown.

Family group: Hawk
Size: 19–25 in (48–63 cm)
Alone or in pairs
Mostly eats mice

Common Nighthawk

(Chordeiles minor)

Although other nightjars feed mainly during the night and roost during the day, the common nighthawk also flies during the day. It is so well camouflaged you aren't likely to see it roosting on the ground or on a branch or roof. Look for it in the air. It is dark gray and its wings are long and pointed with a bold white band across them. Its tail has a fork with a narrow white band near the end. Listen for its nasal PEENT call. It is a summer visitor to most of North America. Unlike other nightjars, it nests on roofs as well as in hollows in the ground. The female lays 2 creamy-buff eggs with gray and brown spots.

Family group: Nightjar
Size: 9–10 in (23–25 cm)
Alone or in groups
Eats flying insects, mostly moths
Also found in open woods and towns

American Kestrel

(Falco sparverius)

This bird of prey is the smallest falcon and is common in most of North America. You might see it in cities as well as in open country. Look for it hovering, or perched on a branch or telephone wire. It has a rust-colored back and a long, rust-colored tail. The male has dark blue inner wings, patches of rust, black, and white on his head, and a black-tipped tail. The female has narrow black bars on her back and tail. She makes a nest in a bare cavity in a tree or building and lays 2 to 7 white eggs heavily spattered with reddish-brown.

Family group:
Falcon
Size: 8–9 in
(20–23 cm)
Usually alone
Mostly eats insects in summer, small mammals in winter

Northern Bobwhite

(Colinus virginianus)

Family group:
Quail (Game bird)
Size: 10 in (25 cm)
Usually feeds and roosts in coveys, except when breeding
Eats seeds on the ground, insects
Also found in open woodlands

This is the only small game bird that is common in the eastern United States. It is brown on top and scaled white underneath. Its sides are striped with reddish-brown. The male's face and eye stripes are white, the female's are cream-colored. In the spring and summer listen for the male's distinctive BOB-WHITE whistle. It makes its nest in a dip in the ground, lines it with grass, and weaves plants over the nest to hide it. The female lays 12 to 24 white eggs.

Grasslands

Vesper Sparrow

(Pooecetes gramineus)
This well-streaked sparrow has less obvious markings on its face than other sparrows. Look for its white eye rings, dark ear patches, and chestnut along its shoulders. When it is flying, look for the white outer tail feathers. This sparrow was called "vesper" because it seemed to sing more often in the evenings. Its song is rich and melodious. It nests in open fields with a lot of weeds and along the side of roads. The female lays 3 to 6 eggs that she incubates alone. In the fall, the bird migrates to the Southern States.
Family group: Sparrow
Size: 6–7 in (15–18 cm)—Usually seen in ones or twos
Eats seeds and insects

Field Sparrow

(Spizella pusilla)

The field sparrow is rustier looking than the vesper sparrow. It has a stubby, bright-pink beak and a rust-colored ring around its eyes. Its call is a sad whistle that rolls into a trill. It breeds in overgrown, bushy fields in the eastern United States and southern Canada. Its nest is a cup of grasses that it makes in a low brush. The female lays 2 to 5 blue-gray eggs spotted with brown. Some birds move south to parts of Florida and Texas for the winter.
Family group: Sparrow
Size: 5–6 in (13–15 cm)—Usually seen in pairs or small flocks
Eats seeds and insects

Killdeer

(Charadrius vociferus)

You will easily see this plover in fields and grasslands. Watch it dart across the ground, stop, then dart off again. Look for the two black bands across its white breast and the black pattern on its face. If it flies off, look for its pointed tail and rust-colored rump. Listen for its repetitive and piercing KILL-DEER call. Its nest is a dip lined with grass and small stones in which the female lays 4 pale tan eggs with black spots. She will pretend that she has been hurt in order to lure egg thieves away from her nest.
Family group: Plover
Size: 9–11 in (23–28 cm)
Alone or in pairs
Eats insects and tiny animals
Also found on freshwater and saltwater mudflats

Black-billed Magpie
(Pica hudsonia)

Magpies are easy to see because of their black-and-white markings and long tail. Its name tells you that this magpie has a black bill. You can see it in the prairies and north into the Rockies and up into southern Alaska. It builds a large dome out of twigs with a cup-shaped nest inside made of mud. The female then lays 5 to 7 gray-green eggs spotted with brown. It steals shiny objects and preys on the eggs and chicks of small birds.

Family group: Crow
Size: 18–19 in (46–48 cm)—Roosts and feeds in flocks
Eats insects, carrion, small animals, and seeds

Ring-necked Pheasant
(Phasianus colchicus)

This very colorful game bird originally came from Asia. You can't miss the male's long, pointed tail, brightly feathered head and neck, and rich brown-and-gold colorings. The female is a less colorful brown and tan, but also has a long tail. Pheasants usually stay hidden in long grass and thickets, but if they are surprised, they fly straight up into the air with their wings whirring loudly. The female lays 6 to 15 dark olive eggs in a hollow in the ground lined with leaves.

Family group:
Game bird
Size: 20–35 in (51–89 cm)
In pairs or small groups
Feeds on the ground on seeds and insects

Dickcissel
(Spiza americana)

Family group: American bunting and grosbeak
Size: 6–7 in (15–18 cm)
Usually flocks
Eats seeds and insects

The male has a black bib and yellow breast. The female has a white chin. Also look for the thick beak, chestnut patch on the wings, and pale yellow stripe across the eyes. It is named after its song, DICK-DICK-DICKCISSEL, although its usual call sounds more like a buzzer. It makes its nest in the prairies eastward and southward, in open fields with tall crops. Its nest is a cup of grasses and leaves where the female lays 3 to 5 pale blue eggs. It spends the winter from southern Mexico to northern South America.

Bobolink
(Dolichonyzx oryzivorus)

In the summer, the male is black with white bands across its wings and rump and a cream-colored hood on the back of its neck. At other times, it looks like the female—streaked with black and tan on top and tan underneath. Look for its sharply pointed wings and tail feathers. It is named for its call, a bubbling and continuous BOB-O-LINK. In the Southern States it is sometimes called the ricebird, because of the large quantities of seeds it eats. This summer visitor may spend the winter as far south as Brazil and Argentina. Its nest is a cup of grasses on the ground where the female lays 4 to 7 gray eggs spotted with brown.
Family group: Blackbird—Size: 7–8 in (18–20 cm)
Eats seeds—Usually in groups, especially in the fall

American Goldfinch
(Carduelis tristis)

This bird is often called the wild canary because in the summer the male is yellow all over except for its black crown, wings, and tail. The female is olive-green on top and pale yellow underneath. Look for the goldfinch's bounding flight and for the two white bands on its black wings. In the winter, the male's face and throat are yellow. His body is brownish on top; the female is gray. Watch for this bird using its delicate beak to pick out the seeds from the head of a thistle and separate them from the fluffy parachutes. The female lays 4 to 6 blue eggs in a nest in a low tree or hedge.

Family group: Finch
Size: 5–6 in (13–15 cm)
Forms large groups, especially in winter
Eats seeds

Eastern & Western Kingbirds
(Tyrannus tyrannus)   *(Tyrannus verticalis)*

The western kingbird (below right) has a yellow belly, gray head and breast, and black tail with narrow white outer edges. The eastern kingbird (below left) has a black crown and almost black back, wings, and tail with a white band at the tip. Its underparts are white. Watch for these birds perching on a branch, post, or telephone wire, waiting to snatch a flying insect. Eastern kingbirds nest in most of North America except the far West and Southwest. The western kingbird is most common in the western United States. Both build nests of twigs and lay 3 to 5 white eggs spotted with brown and black.

Family group:
Tyrant flycatcher
Size: 8–9 in (20–23 cm)
Alone or in groups
Eats flying insects

Eastern & Western Bluebirds

(Sialia sialis)
(Sialia mexicana)

Both of these birds are blue on top and rust-colored underneath, although the western bluebird is darker than the eastern bluebird and has a gray belly instead of a white one. The western bluebird also is chestnut on its upper back. The females are gray instead of blue on top. Look for these birds perching on twigs and branches. Watch them drop off the branches to catch insects on the ground or in the air. Listen for their calls. The eastern bluebird's is a melodic CHUR-LEE, the western bluebird's is a deep, repeated FEW. Both birds make their nests in holes in trees or in nest boxes. They lay between 3 and 7 pale blue eggs.

Family group: Thrush
Size: 6–7 in (15–18 cm)
Usually in pairs or small groups
Eats insects and fruit

Horned Lark

(Eremophila alpestris)
This bird is brown-and-tan streaked on top, whitish underneath. The black "horns" are often hard to see, but the black markings on its face, neck, and crown are easy to spot. When it is flying, look for its black tail with white outer feathers. The horned lark likes to breed in the short grass in the prairies and the tundra. Its nest is a simple cup of grasses on the ground where the female lays 2 to 5 greenish eggs speckled with brown. In the winter, you may see it in empty fields or on the shore.
Family group: Lark
Size: 7–8 in (18–20 cm)—Usually seen in groups
Also found on shores—Eats seeds and insects on the ground

Eastern & Western Meadowlarks

(Sturnella magna)
(Sturnella neglecta)

Family group: Blackbird
Size: 9–10 in (23–25 cm)
Usually seen in pairs or small flocks
Eats insects and seeds on the ground

Both of these birds are streaked on top and yellow underneath. Look for the V-shaped black band on the breast. These birds are not shy and you can get quite close to them. Although they look alike, they sound very different. The eastern meadowlark's call is a SEE-YOU-SEE-YER whistle. The western meadowlark's song sounds like something bubbling. Their nests are grassy cups with a domed roof, hidden in the grass. Both females lay 3 to 7 white eggs spotted with brown.

Out in the Wild

When you go on a serious bird-watching expedition, you must dress properly. If it is cold, dress warmly, as you will be spending a lot of time keeping very still. Also, try to wear clothes that do not make noise as you move. Dress in dull colors that will blend in with the ground and bushes. Dull greens and browns are good. Anything bright will alert the birds. If it is snowy, of course, white is best.

Take a notebook, pencils, eraser, this book, and binoculars with you. You will get the most out of your expedition if you keep a record of what you see. Do your best not to let the birds know you are there. Making a blind for yourself will help.

Making a blind

If you know of a good place to watch birds but can't get close enough without bothering them, then why not build your own blind?

1 **Find four wooden posts** about 5 ft (1.5 m) long for the uprights, and four boards about 3 ft (1 m) long for the top.
2 **You will also need a piece of canvas** measuring about 13 ft (4 m) square to cover a blind for one person.
3 **Paint or dye the canvas** with green-and-brown splotches to camouflage it. Leave a flap for the door and cut out two narrow slits for windows.

4 **To build the blind,** hammer the upright posts firmly into the ground. Ask an adult to help you with this.

5 **Tie the top boards to the posts,** as shown in the picture. Find something to sit on as well.

6 **Hang the canvas over the top.** Put some large stones around the bottom of the canvas to stop it from flapping in the wind.
7 **Leave your blind empty for a day or two,** so the birds can get used to it before you use it.
8 **Once you begin using it,** you must remain quiet. The slightest noise will frighten off any birds you may be watching.

Hiding in a car

A car makes a good blind, too. Be prepared to wait for a little while after the car has stopped for the birds to get used to it. Keep very quiet and still inside. The birds can easily see you through the windows. Roll down the windows a little so that the inside of the glass does not steam up.

Footprints in plaster

In wet weather or after a thaw, look for some clear bird footprints in the mud in your yard. You can make a cast of them.

1 **Bend a strip of thick paper into an oval** to make a mold. Fasten the ends with a paper clip.

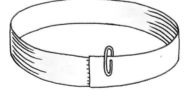

2 **Mix up some plaster of Paris** according to the instructions on the box.

3 **Put your mold over the footprint** and pour in the plaster of Paris mixture.

4 **Let the cast harden** before you lift the mold and the plaster.

5 **Wash off the dirt.** Allow a few days for the plaster to set firmly. You can paint or varnish the footprint.

Field sketches

When you see a bird you don't recognize, don't try to look it up in your book. The bird will fly off before you can find it. Instead, make a quick sketch in your notebook with a pencil. You can make a good drawing of the main features by using the simple shapes shown above to draw its outline. Then add the most important details:
- Where are the main patches of color?
- What shape is its tail?
- Can you see the shape of its beak?

Make a note of what the bird is doing and any other information that will help you identify it. Now you can look it up in your book.

A field notebook

Use your field sketches as the basis for a field notebook. For each bird you see, write down the date, where you saw it, and what kind of habitat it was in. If you know the bird already, you can still record what it was doing, whether it was alone or in a group, and what other birds were nearby.

Deserts

This section covers the mesquite or cactus deserts of the southwestern United States, and sagebrush deserts. They have little rain and are very hot in the summer. You won't be surprised to find cactus, yuccas, and other desert plants growing here.

One of the reasons that birds can survive well in deserts is because they can fly over large areas looking for water. Some have adapted extremely well—the black-throated sparrow lives in some of the most inhospitable deserts of the United States. Others, like the vermilion flycatcher, keep to the scrub around ponds and streams on the edge of the deserts.

Some birds move to more fertile areas during the long hot season, but others breed and nest in the desert. They usually breed during the short rainy season. Then the desert blooms with wild flowers and insects, providing lots of food to feed the chicks. The picture shows eight kinds of birds from this section. How many can you identify?

Inca dove, Costa's hummingbird, elf owl, scaled quails, chihuahuan ravens, greater roadrunner, black-throated sparrow, cactus wren

Elf Owl
(Microthene whitneyi)

This tiny owl lives in the deserts and dry woods in the southwestern United States and western Mexico. It has a short tail and is striped and spotted with brown, tan, and chestnut. Like all owls, it has a round head and its yellow eyes point forward. It is active at dawn, dusk, and through the night. Its call is a group of high CHIRRUPS. It often nests in trees or in old woodpecker holes in cacti and lays 3 to 4 white eggs. During the day it roosts in these holes.

Family group: Owl
Size: 5–6 in
(13–15 cm)
Usually alone
Feeds mainly on insects
Summer visitor

Greater Roadrunner

(Geococcyx californianus)

This is another well-known bird that lives on the ground and likes running more than flying. It has a long, black tail and is heavily streaked with brown and white. It has a large, heavy, black beak and bushy crest. Look for it speeding across the desert on its long, strong legs. It builds a neat saucer-shaped nest among the thorns of a cactus plant and lays 2 to 6 white eggs. The female incubates the eggs as soon as they are laid, so the eggs do not all hatch at the same time.

Family group: Cuckoo
Size: 22–23 in (56–58 cm)
Usually alone or in loose groups
Eats insects, lizards, snakes, rodents, and small birds

Chihuahuan Raven
(Corvus cryptoleucus)

Ravens look a lot like crows, although they are larger and their tails are wedge-shaped. But you aren't likely to find crows in the dry lands of the southwestern United States where the chihuahuan raven lives. To be sure, listen for its call, which is a long drawn-out croak. The chihuahuan raven used to be called the white-necked raven because its heavy black ruff covers white neck feathers. Its nest is a platform of twigs which it uses again and adds to year after year until it becomes very big. The female lays 3 to 6 olive-green eggs, spotted with brown.

Family group: Crow
Size: 19–20 in (48–51 cm)
Forms large flocks
Preys on insects, small animals, plus carrion and fruit

Deserts

Costa's Hummingbird
(Calypte costae)

You will only see this tiny bird in the waterless parts of southern California and Arizona, and many move farther south for the winter. It is green on top and white underneath. The male has a violet-colored head which may look black in weak light. You are most likely to see this bird feeding with its long, needlelike beak from a cactus flower. It hovers as it feeds, its wings beating so fast they hum. The female lays 2 white eggs in a tiny nest built across the low branch of a bush.

Family group: Hummingbird
Size: 3–4 in (8–10 cm)
Alone or in small groups
Eats nectar of flowers and insects

Inca Dove
(Columbina inca)

Doves are the same shape as pigeons, but are smaller. The feathers of the Inca dove form a very clear, scaly pattern above and below. Look for the chestnut coloring on its wings when it is flying and for the white outer feathers on its long, gray tail. Listen for its HOOH-HOOH call. Its nest is a platform of twigs in which the female lays 2 creamy-white eggs. Like other doves, it has a long breeding season, with at least 2 and sometimes 5 broods of young each year.

Family group: Dove
Size: 8 in (20 cm)—Forms flocks—Eats seeds

Scaled Quail
(Callipepla squamata)

Quails are chubby, chickenlike birds. The scaled quail is found only in the semi-deserts of the western and southwestern United States. It is sometimes known as "cotton-top" because of its pale, white-tipped crest. It is gray-brown on top and rust-colored underneath. Its breast and side feathers are black on the edges, making it look scaly in front. It feeds on the ground and likes to run rather than to fly. Its nest is a hollow in the ground, hidden in prickly plants, in which the female lays 5 to 16 tan eggs with brown spots.

Family group: Quail (Game bird)
Size: 10–12 in (25–30 cm)
In coveys, except when breeding
Feeds from the ground on seeds and some insects

Cactus Wren
(Campylorhynchus brunneicapillus)

This is our largest wren and is very noisy. Its back and wings are streaked and banded in white, black, and dark brown. Its white breast has heavy black spots. Look for its long, heavy beak and long, rounded tail. You are most likely to find it in cactus country. Listen for its harsh CHUG-CHUG-CHUG, which you can hear at any time of day. Its nest looks like a haystack among the thorns of a cholla or yucca. In it the female lays 2 to 5 pinkish eggs spotted with brown.
Family group: Wren
Size: 8–9 in (20–23 cm)—Pairs or family groups
Eats insects, spiders, and some fruits and seeds

Black-throated Sparrow
(Amphispiza bilineata)

This bird lives in some of the hottest and driest deserts in North America, from Oregon and Wyoming to central Texas. It is brown on top and white underneath. It is named for the black patch on its throat. Look for the two white streaks on its face, too. It builds its nest of stems and grasses placed in a bush or cactus. The female lays 3 or 4 white eggs washed with pale blue.
Family group: Sparrow
Size: 5–6 in (13–15 cm)
Often in small groups
Eats seeds of desert plants and insects

Abert's Towhee
(Pipilo aberti)

This bird is one of a group of long-tailed ground birds—the towhees. It is brown on top and creamy-colored underneath. Look for its black face and long tail. It lives in the dry woodlands and scrub of southeastern California and Arizona. It is shy and secretive, so listen for its call—a sharp POLK—and its song, a rolling trill of POLK notes. Its nest is a cup of stems and plants built in a low bush. The female lays 1 to 4 bluish-green eggs spotted with brown.
Family group: Finch
Size: 9–10 in (23–25 cm)—Alone or in pairs
Feeds on seeds and insects on the ground
Also found in farmlands and near suburbs in the Southwest

Vermilion Flycatcher
(Pyrocephalus rubinus)

Look for this bird where deserts meet trees and streams. The male is hard to miss with its bright red crown and underparts and brown upper parts. The female has an orange-red wash on her belly, a streaked breast, and tan-brown upper parts. This bird likes bare, dry ground, but doesn't breed much farther north than the Mexican border. Listen for the male's soft PIT-A-SEE song. It builds its nest in a tree about 8 to 20 feet (2.4 to 6.1 meters) high and lays 2 to 4 off-white eggs spotted with brown.

Family group: Tyrant flycatcher
Size: 5–6 in (13–15 cm)
Alone or in pairs
Eats flying insects

Long-distance Flyers

You may already be familiar with the comings and goings of robins and dark-eyed juncos around your home, but look out for different birds in spring and fall. They may be pausing to rest or feed as they migrate (or move home) from one part of the country to another.

Flying uses a lot of energy, so they need to keep filling up with food. Some species, such as hawks, swallows, and gulls, move in daylight. Others, including warblers and some species of sparrows, move at night.

Where do they go?

Some birds have quite spectacular journeys. The Arctic tern travels farthest, from its breeding grounds in the Arctic to spend the winter in the Antarctic. In the fall, the American golden-plover flies from northern Canada to Argentina. It rarely stops to rest; it can fly up to 2,500 miles (4,023 kilometers) without pausing.

Why do birds migrate? Many birds that breed in North America spend the winters in the warmer south. There they can escape the cold weather. Others may migrate to fresh sources of food, but no one can fully explain the regular movement of some birds in spring and fall.

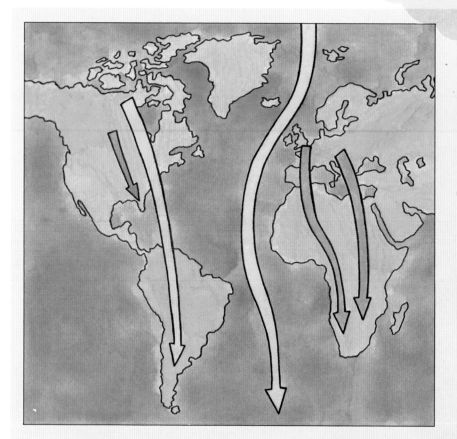

RUBY-THROATED HUMMINGBIRD
3-4 in (8-10 cm) long, it migrates 1,500 miles (2,414 km) south to Florida

ARCTIC TERN
17 in (43 cm) long, it migrates 11,000 miles (17,703 km) to the Antarctic

AMERICAN GOLDEN-PLOVER
10–11 in (25–28 cm) long, it migrates 6,000 miles (9,656 km) to South America

BARN SWALLOW
6-7 in (15-18 cm) long, it migrates 7,000 miles (11,265 km) to Africa

Finding their way

How birds migrate is even more mysterious, but they probably use the sun or the light of the stars to find their way. Many birds migrate along the coasts. This is safer than flying across oceans and probably helps them to stay on course. But on foggy nights, they may become confused by the long flashes of light from lighthouses and fly straight toward them. To stop birds from flying into them, some lighthouses have changed to using short flashes only.

Bird warning

Migrating birds that are just passing through can be confused by large windows. They may try to fly through them and stun themselves. You can help by hanging a warning in your window. A hawk shape works well because most birds keep well away from hawks.

1 **Trace the blue hawk shape** you see here onto a piece of thin paper with a pencil.
2 **Glue it on to a large piece of thin cardboard** like an empty cereal box or carton. Carefully cut around the edges with scissors.
3 **Color the hawk shape black** using a crayon or marker. The blacker you can make it, the better.
4 **Attach about 2 feet (61 centimeters) of string** to the head of the hawk with adhesive tape and thumb-tack it to the top of your window frame.
5 **If you can attach it to the outside of your window,** it will move about in the wind and look more realistic. But first cover it in plastic to keep the rain off it. If you use black plastic, it will save you from having to color in the shape.
6 **You can also hang glittering or tinkling objects** in a window. Tape long streamers of aluminum foil to the top of the frame or hang up some wind chimes.
7 **Or you could tack some light, see-through material** over the glass to reduce the reflections. This need be up only during the danger periods in the spring and fall.

Evergreen Forests

These forests form a wide belt across North America. A form of this habitat is also found down the Pacific coast along the Rocky Mountains. The trees you are most likely to see here are pines, spruces, hemlocks, firs, junipers, and tamaracks. All these trees are coniferous, which means that they produce cones containing seeds and they mostly have needles for their leaves.

Evergreen forests also grow in a band high up in the mountains. In these places the summers are usually cool and the winters very cold. Many birds come to these forests to breed, then fly south to spend the winter in warmer places. You may find some of the same birds in broadleaf forests and on evergreen trees in mixed woodlands, too.

Many small birds live in the evergreen forests. They feed on seeds and insects and roost and nest in the trees. Grosbeaks and finches have strong, sturdy beaks which they use to pick out the seeds from fir cones. Crossbills have special crossed beaks for picking out the seeds of pine cones.

You will hear many fine songs in these forests, from warblers and thrushes in particular. Learning to recognize their songs will help you identify them. The picture shows seven kinds of birds from this section. How many can you identify?

Red crossbill, pine grosbeak, spruce grouse, pine siskins, western tanager, hermit thrushes, golden-crowned kinglet

Evergreen Forests

Pine Grosbeak
(Pinicola enucleator)

**Family group:
Finch
Size: 9–10 in
(23–25 cm)
Alone or in small
groups
Eats seeds
Also found in
other habitats,
including suburban
yards in winter**

You can tell this is a finch by its chunky beak and the way it flies up and down, rather than straight from one perch to another. The male is red all over except for his long black tail and wings. Look for the two white bands on the wings. The female is a warm buff-orange on the head but is gray where the male is red. You might see this bird in the north of Canada and farther south in the east and west into the United States. The female lays 2 to 5 blue-green eggs spotted with brown.

Red Crossbill
(Loxia curvirostra)

In the spring and summer, you are most likely to see this bird in the forests of Canada and the western mountains, but in the winter, you might see it almost anywhere. The male is red with brownish wings and tail. The female is greenish-yellow instead of red. It can be hard to see its crossed beak, which it uses to pick the seeds out of pine cones. When it is flying, look for its short, notched tail and listen for its clear KIP call. It makes its nests nearly all year and lays 3 or 4 pale green eggs with purplish spots.

**Family group:
Finch
Size: 6–7 in
(15–18 cm)
Alone or in small
groups
Eats pine seeds
and insects
Also found in
other habitats**

White-winged Crossbill
(Loxia leucoptera)

This bird is similar to the red crossbill (see opposite page) except that it has two bold white bands on its wings. Look for the crossed beak and short notched tail, too. When it is flying, you might hear its CHET-CHET call. It is most common in the evergreen forests of Canada and the northern Rockies, but it and the red crossbill may show up almost anywhere there are pine cones. It can breed almost all the year around and lays 2 to 4 pale green eggs spotted with brown.

Family group: Finch
Size: 6–7 in (15–18 cm)—Alone or in small groups
Eats pine seeds and insects
Also found in other habitats, especially in winter

Pine Siskin
(Carduelis pinus)

In most of the United States, you will see this bird only in the winter. Most fly north to Canada to breed, although some stay in the western mountains all year. It is streaked brown on top and brown and white underneath. It has a thin beak for a finch. When it is flying, look for the yellow on its wings. It makes its nest of twigs and grass and decorates it with lichen. The female lays 3 or 4 blue eggs spotted with brown. Although it almost always nests in evergreen trees, it often visits other trees, particularly alders.

Family group: Finch
Size: 4–5 in
(10–13 cm)
Usually in flocks
Eats seeds

Family group:
Wood warbler
Size: 5–6 in
(13–15 cm)
Usually alone
Eats insects, seeds,
and berries

Pine Warbler
(Dendroica pinus)

You can tell this warbler is different from the finches by its longer tail and beak and its pleasant trilling song. It is olive-green on top and yellow underneath. It has two white bands on its olive-green wings. You might see it in pine woods in the Eastern States. Watch for it crawling along the branches and trunks of pine trees, searching in the bark for insects. Its nest is a cup of grasses and stems lined with pine needles in which the female lays 3 to 5 white eggs spotted with brown.

Magnolia Warbler
(Dendroica magnolia)

This bird has a gray head, yellow underparts streaked with black, and black wings and tail. Look for the yellow rump and white bands on the wings and the white patches on the tail. The male has a black eye mask. It breeds across Canada and southward into the Appalachians. It makes its nest in young spruce and hemlock trees and lays 3 to 5 white eggs speckled with brown. It always migrates across the Eastern States to spend the winter in Central America.

Family group: Wood warbler
Size: 5 in (13 cm)
Usually alone
Eats insects
Summer visitor

Western Tanager
(Piranga ludoviciana)

You are most likely to see this stunning bird in the spring or summer in the high forests of the western mountains. It is yellow underneath with a black back, tail, and wings. Look for the male's bright red head and the two yellow bands on its wings. Its song is a harsh whistle. It builds its nest of twigs and grasses in an evergreen tree and lines it with hair. The female lays 3 to 5 pale blue eggs with light brown spots.

Family group: Tanager
Size: 7–8 in (18–20 cm)
Usually alone
Eats insects and berries
Also found in other habitats
Summer visitor

Hermit Thrush *(Catharus guttatus)*

This tiny thrush is brown on top with a rust-red tail and white underneath with brown-and-gray spots. It spends most of its time on the ground searching in plants for food, but it likes to sing from the top of a tall tree. Listen for its famous flutelike phrases. It breeds in woods across Canada and the Rockies and then migrates to the southern United States and Atlantic States for the winter. It makes its nest among roots on the ground and lays 3 to 4 greenish-blue eggs.

Family group: Thrush
Size: 6–7 in (15–18 cm)
Usually alone
Eats insects and berries
Also found in mixed woodlands

Yellow-rumped Warbler
(Dendroica coronata)

**Family group:
Wood warbler
Size: 5–6 in
(13–15 cm)
Alone or in groups
Eats insects
Also found in
mixed woodlands**

This bird is gray on top, streaked with black and white underneath with a black breast band. Look for the yellow patches on the rump and side. The male also has a yellow crown and some have a yellow throat. You might see this bird in many kinds of woodlands in the North and West in the spring and summer and in the South and East in the winter. It builds its nest out of twigs and grasses in pine trees and the female lays 4 or 5 white eggs that are spotted with brown.

Evening Grosbeak
(Coccothraustes vespertinus)

This finch is easy to see. It is noisy, large, and stocky with a stout, pale beak. The male is yellow with a black tail and black-and-white markings on its wings. The female is a grayer color. In the spring and summer it breeds in Canada and southward into the Rockies. It builds its nest in an evergreen tree and lays 3 to 5 greenish-blue eggs with brown spots. It spends the winter in much of the rest of the United States, where large flocks will come to birdfeeders to eat sunflower seeds.

**Family group:
Finch
Size: 8 in (20 cm)
May form large
flocks in winter
Eats seeds
Also found in
mixed woods**

Spruce Grouse
(Falcipennis canadensis)

You may see this chubby game bird along the sides of roads or perched in trees in forests from Alaska to Nova Scotia. The male is easy to see with his black fantail. Look for his black throat and breast bordered with white. You might be lucky and see him trying to attract a female. He spreads his tail, lifts the red wattles above his eyes, and beats his wings. Their nest is a well-hidden hollow in the ground. The female lays 4 to 10 deep cream-colored eggs spotted with brown.

Family group: Grouse
Size: 16 in (41 cm)
Usually in groups
Feeds on the ground
on seeds and insects

Family group: Owl
Size: 17–18 in
(43–46 cm)
Hunts alone
Eats rodents and
other small
animals

Spotted Owl
(Strix occidentalis)

This owl is brown with white spots on top and underneath. It hunts at night and so is hard to see in the daytime. Listen for flocks of small songbirds mobbing it as it roosts during the day. Look for owl pellets on the ground. The spotted owl is becoming scarcer as the wooded gullies and damp forests where it lives in the West and Southwest are destroyed. It usually makes its nest in a hole or a tree or cliff but sometimes uses a hawk's old nest. The female lays 2 to 4 white eggs.

Golden-crowned Kinglet

(Regulus satrapa)
This tiny, chubby bird is greenish on top and whitish underneath. Look for the orange-red crown in the male and yellow crown in the female. Watch it nervously twitch its wings. It likes to eat high up in trees so listen for its high, thin SEE-SEE-SEE notes. It breeds in evergreen forests in Canada, the western mountains, and parts of the northern United States. It builds its nest of moss and feathers and lays 5 to 11 white eggs spotted with brown. It migrates to all parts of the United States for the winter.
Family group: Warbler—Size 3–4 in (8–10 cm)
Usually in ones or twos—Eats insects

Red-breasted Nuthatch

(Sitta canadensis)

This little, short-tailed bird is rust-colored underneath and gray on top. Look for the black cap and black stripe through its eyes. You may find it in evergreen forests in a lot of North America, but in most of the United States, you will see it only in the winter. Watch it climb up, down, and around tree trunks and branches looking for food. Listen for its call—a high-pitched HENNK. It makes a hole in a rotting tree stump, where it builds its nest and lays 4 to 7 white eggs spotted with reddish-brown.

Family group:
Nuthatch
Size: 4–5 in (10–13 cm)
Often in flocks, especially in winter
Eats insects and nuts

Ruby-crowned Kinglet

(Regulus calendula)

This tiny bird also nervously twitches its wings and looks a lot like the golden-crowned kinglet except that its face doesn't have that bird's white-and-black stripes. The male has a red crest, but this might be hard to see. Like the golden-crowned kinglet, the best way to find it is by its thin, high-pitched SEE-SEE-SEE call or its typical DIDIT. It breeds in Canada and in the Rockies. Its nest is a ball of mosses held together with cobwebs and usually built high in an evergreen tree. The female lays 5 to 11 white eggs spotted with brown.

Family group:
Warbler
Size: 4–5 in (10–13 cm)
Often in small groups
Eats insects and some berries

Helping Birds in Danger

The best way to help endangered species is to join a wildlife group that is working to save them. They need your money, and they need as many people as possible to become aware of the problems. You can do your part as well by explaining the problems to other people.

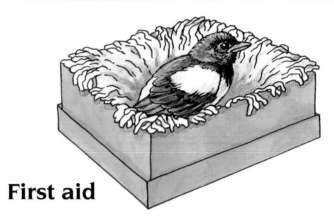

First aid

If you find a bird that has been hurt by flying into a window, take it indoors and place it in a medium-sized box with a lid. Before putting the bird in the box, punch a few air holes in the lid. Don't handle the bird without gloves. Also, don't handle it any more than you have to. After a few hours rest, it will probably have recovered enough for you to let it go. For more serious injuries, call the local wildlife society. If you find a chick helpless on the ground, but alive, what should you do?

1 **Don't touch it** until you have watched and listened to check whether the parents are nearby, looking after the chick from a distance.
2 **When you are sure they are not, then make a nest for the bird** in a small box with shredded kitchen towels or tissues. Keep it very quiet. Then call the local wildlife society or conservation officer to ask what to do.

Get involved

Find out whether there is a local group involved in wildlife conservation. If you join it, you can help with fund-raising and other local activities.

1 **Listen for particular issues.** Is there an area of land important to wildlife that is being threatened by construction? As towns or cities grow, woods may be cut down and marshes drained to make more land for buildings. You can write to government officials asking them to help your cause.
2 **Visit as many bird sanctuaries as possible.** Not only will you enjoy seeing the birds, but you will also see what is being done to help them.

Rescuing an oiled bird

A particular danger for sea birds is oil, either spilled by accident or emptied by tankers into the sea. Once a bird's feathers are covered in oil, it cannot swim or fly, so it cannot catch food and will soon starve to death. Even a small amount of oil can do a lot of harm. If the bird tries to clean itself by preening, it may swallow enough oil to kill it. If you find a live bird covered in oil, do not try to clean it yourself. Contact a local bird group or vet who will know who can deal with it.

Keeping track

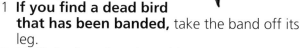

Scientists try to keep track of migrating birds by watching them on radar and also by putting an aluminum or plastic band around one leg. The band does not hurt the bird in any way.

1 **If you find a dead bird that has been banded,** take the band off its leg.
2 **Mail the band** to the address given on it.
3 **Enclose a note** about when, where, and how you found the dead bird.

A bird-friendly garden

You can make your own small bird sanctuary in your garden with your parents' help.

1 **Ask if you can plant the trees and shrubs** that birds particularly like. Elder, dogwood, hawthorn, cotoneaster, and holly are good ones to begin with. Any tree or shrub with fruit or berries will soon bring birds into your garden.
2 **Ask if you can make a special corner** where you can let the weeds grow. Bristle grass, panic grass, and even ragweed all have seeds that birds like to eat. Sweet-smelling shrubs will attract insects—and insect-eating birds.
3 **Marigolds will attract birds** if their flower heads are left to go to seed in fall and winter.
4 **Watch carefully yourself.** What plants do the birds visit most? Which ones do they ignore? You will know which ones to keep next year!
5 **If you plant thick vines,** like honeysuckle and ivy, you may find birds nesting in them, too.

Seashores & Marshes

Seashore habitats include sandy beaches, rocky beaches, and sea cliffs. Many birds come inland to breed in the salt marshes behind the shores.

Some of these birds, like the common tern, you will mainly see flying over the sea, but they land on the shore to roost and nest. Others feed on the beach creatures or, like herring gulls, are scavengers.

Salt marshes form behind the seashore where rivers meet the sea and plants begin to grow. When the tide goes out, it may uncover large areas of mudflat. Few kinds of plants grow in these brackish waters, but many birds flourish here. Ducks and geese come here from inland waters, and shorebirds find shelter here, too. In fall and winter, look for migrating birds, such as swallows, thrushes, warblers, and hawks. The picture shows seven kinds of birds from this section. How many can you identify?

Ring-billed gull, laughing gull, brown pelicans, semipalmated plover, sanderlings, common terns, ruddy turnstone

Common Tern
(Sterna hirundo)

Terns are generally smaller than gulls and have pointed bills. The common tern is pale gray on top and lighter gray underneath. The top of its head is black, and it has an orange-red bill with a black tip. Its legs are orange-red, too. Listen for its low, drawn-out KEE-ARR call. You are most likely to see it on the coast as it migrates from its breeding grounds in southern Canada and the northeastern United States coast. Its nest is a hollow in which the female lays 3 or 4 whitish to brownish eggs speckled with brown.

**Family group: Tern
Size: 12–15 in (30–38 cm)
Usually in groups
Dives for fish
Migrates to South America in the winter**

Herring Gull
(Larus argentatus)

This is the standard sea gull. Adult herring gulls are white with gray backs. Their gray wings have black tips. Look for their pink legs and the red spot on their yellow bill. Young birds are mottled brown. Herring gulls get along very well with people. They scavenge whatever they can from garbage dumps and along the shore. You will easily hear their loud KYOW-KYOW calls. Herring gulls nest inland and along the coasts across Alaska, most of Canada, and the eastern United States. Each female lays 2 to 4 pale green eggs spattered with brown.
**Family group: Gull—Size: 25 in (64 cm)
Usually found in large groups—Eats fish and scavenges**

Laughing Gull
(Larus atricilla)

You can see this gull anywhere along the Atlantic Coast, south of Maine, and the Gulf Coast. It has a large, red bill, black legs, and dark gray wings with large black edges. When it is breeding, it has a black head, but in the winter this fades to a dark patch at the back of the head and around the eyes. Its call sounds like a low chuckle or laugh. It nests in salt marshes. Its nest is a hollow lined with grass, in which the female lays 3 olive-brown eggs spotted with brown. Both birds incubate the eggs.
**Family group: Gull
Size: 17 in (43 cm)—Eats fish
Usually found in flocks**

Ring-billed Gull *(Larus delawarensis)*

This gull looks a lot like the herring gull but is a little bit smaller. You can tell them apart by the color of their legs and their bills. The ring-billed gull has yellow legs and a black vertical stripe on its bill. You are most likely to see it in marshes and lakes in the summer and along the coast with herring gulls in the winter. It nests on islands in inland lakes and the sea. Its nest is a pile of grasses in which the female lays 2 to 8 tan-colored eggs spotted with brown.
**Family group: Gull
Size: 19 in (48 cm)
Found in large groups
Eats fish and scavenges**

Also found inland

Brown Pelican
(Pelecanus occidentalis)

Pelicans are easy to recognize because of their huge bills and pouches. The adult brown pelican is silvery-brown with a large, dark brown bill and pouch. Look at the color of its neck. When its back is chestnut, the bird is breeding or feeding chicks. Young birds are brown and whitish with dark upper parts. This is the only pelican that dives into the water for its food. Its nest is a big heap of sticks in which the female lays 2 to 4 white eggs.

Family group: Pelican
Size: 45–54 in (114–137 cm)
Usually found in groups—Eats fish

Red-throated Loon
(Gavia stellata)

The red-throated loon is the smallest kind of loon, and it usually holds its bill pointed upward. You are most likely to see it on the coasts in the winter, when its face is white and its back is spotted with white. Loons dive under the water and are excellent swimmers. They migrate to the far north to breed. Then they come onto land and nest close to the water's edge. They lay 2 olive-brown eggs speckled with brown or black.

Family group: Loon
Size: 25 in (64 cm)
Migrates in loose groups
Dives for fish

Willet
(Catoptrophorus semipalmatus)

The willet is large, chubby, and easy to see. Like all sandpipers, it has a long bill and long legs. It is gray and white in the winter and has heavy bands and streaks in the summer. Look for the black-and-white bands on its wings when it flies. It is a noisy bird; its call sometimes sounds like PILL WILL-WILLET. It nests in marshes and on inland lakes and lays 4 buff-olive eggs spotted with brown. It moves to the coast for the winter.

Family group: Sandpiper
Size: 14–17 in (36–43 cm)
Forms small flocks in the winter
Feeds in shallow water and on mudflats on small animals

Ruddy Turnstone
(Arenaria interpres)

This chunky bird has a short bill and short legs. Its wings and back are black and chestnut in the summer and gray in the winter. Look for the pattern of white and dark colors on its back and wings when it flies. It turns over shells and stones with its bill, looking for food underneath. It nests in the far north, laying 4 olive-green eggs blotched with brown. In the fall, it flies south and can be seen along every coastline in the world, except Asia, all through the year.

Family group: Turnstone
Size: 8–10 in (20–25 cm)
Often in small or loose flocks
Eats small animals on the shore

Sanderling
(Calidris alba)

Look for this little bird in the winter along the North American coasts. It is pale gray, paler than any other sandpiper. Its bill and legs are black. In the summer, it has a chestnut head, back, and breast. You are most likely to see flocks of sanderlings running up and down the beach, keeping just in front of the surf and looking for tiny marine animals left behind by the waves. It nests in the far north, laying 3 or 4 olive-green eggs spotted with brown.

Family group: Sandpiper
Size: 7–9 in (18–23 cm)
Usually in small flocks
Eats mollusks and shellfish

Semipalmated Plover
(Charadrius semipalmatus)

Plovers dart across the ground, stop suddenly, and then dart off again. They have short beaks and long legs. Several kinds of plovers are brown or tan on top and white underneath with black-and-white head and breast markings. You should look carefully at these markings to tell this plover apart from others. Listen for its CHUR-LEE call. It nests in the far north on tide flats, where the female lays 4 buff-colored eggs spotted with brown. In the fall, it migrates south along the coasts.

Family group: Plover
Size: 7–8 in (18–20 cm)
Often found in small, loose groups
Eats tiny animals from the surface of the wet sand or mud

Lakes, Rivers, & Marshes

These habitats all have open stretches of fresh water, often with shallower water around the edges, with many water plants and shrubs and trees growing nearby.

Diving birds, such as the common merganser, use their webbed feet to swim in the open water and dive down deep for their food. Dabbling ducks, such as American wigeons, swim too but feed on the surface. They strain the water through their large, flat bills and often "up-end" to search the water just below the surface.

Long-legged birds like herons wade in the shallow water around the edge. Then they pounce on fish with their long beaks. The picture shows eight kinds of birds from this section. How many can you identify?

Wood duck, great blue heron, belted kingfisher, common merganser, osprey, American wigeon, great egret, Canada geese (flying in V in background)

Greater Yellowlegs
(Tringa melanoleuca)

This bird is named after its long yellow legs. It looks gray on top, although it is really spotted black and white. It is white underneath, with some streaks on its neck and breast. Its call is a loud, descending WHEE-WHEE-WHEW. Its nest is a well-lined scrape in which the female lays 4 buff-colored eggs spotted with brown. In the fall, it flies south and is a regular sight in salt marshes and on mudflats and lakes.

Family group: Sandpiper
Size: 12–15 in (30–38 cm)—Found singly or in loose flocks
Feeds in shallow water—Also found in freshwater marshes

Lesser Yellowlegs
(Tringa flavipes)

This bird looks a lot like the greater yellowlegs except that it is smaller, more elegant, and its bill is shorter. Both birds are gray on top and white underneath. When they fly, you can see their white rumps behind their gray wings. The lesser yellowlegs even sounds like the larger bird, but its YOO-YOO call is softer and shorter. The lesser yellowlegs nests on the ground, away from water, usually in clearings. The female lays 4 buff-colored eggs, spotted with brown. In the fall it migrates as far south as South America.

Family group: Sandpiper
Size: 9–11 in (23–28 cm)—Found singly or in flocks
Feeds in shallow water—Also found in freshwater marshes

Family group: Heron
Size: 35–41 in (89–104 cm)
Often in loose groups
Eats fish
Also found in saltwater marshes

Great Egret
(Ardea alba)

You can tell this is a heron by its long, dark legs and long, yellow bill. Look for the distinctive way it kinks its neck when it is resting. It is the largest white heron species and the most common worldwide. It was once hunted for its plumes. It nests in thickets and reeds on the edge of marshes. Its nest is a platform of sticks built in a tree or among the reeds. The female lays 3 to 5 pale blue eggs. It flies to the warmer southern coasts for the winter.

Snowy Egret
(Egretta thula)

Herons have long legs and long necks. They fly with their necks tucked in, unlike cranes, which stretch theirs out. The snowy egret is thin and elegant, with white feathers. Look for its black bill, black legs, and yellow feet, although its feet could look black if covered with mud. When it is breeding, it has a crest of plumes, which made it prized by hunters long ago. Now this bird is protected. Its nest is a platform of twigs in a tree or tall bush next to a marsh. The female lays 3 to 6 pale blue eggs.

Family group: Heron
Size: 24 in (61 cm)
Often in loose flocks
Eats small mud-dwelling creatures
Also found in freshwater marshes

Great Blue Heron
(Ardea herodias)

This is our largest heron. It is mainly gray with a white head and black crest. You might see it wading on its long legs by the side of lakes or marshes, darting out to grab a fish in its daggerlike bill. Or you may see it preening itself with its comblike middle claw. When it flies, it tucks its neck back into its shoulders. It makes its nest of twigs near the top of a tree, returning and adding to the same nest year after year. The female lays 3 to 6 pale blue eggs.

Family group: Heron
Size: 47 in (119 cm)
Alone or in loose groups
Feeds in shallow water on fish and frogs

Tundra Swan
(Cygnus columbianus)

Four kinds of swan live in North America. You can tell them apart by the color of their bills. The tundra swan has a black bill, and there is usually a small spot of yellow in front of the eyes. When it rests, it holds its long neck straight up from its breast. It makes its nest in marshes in the far north of Canada and Alaska, and in the fall, it moves south to ponds and lakes near the United States coasts. It makes a nest of grass and moss near the water and lays 4 to 6 creamy-white eggs.

Family group: Swan
Size: 56 in (142 cm)
Forms flocks in winter and during migration
Feeds in water on aquatic plants and small crustaceans

Canada Goose
(Branta canadensis)

Family group: Goose
Size: 22–36 in (56–91 cm)
Found in flocks
Feeds in water and grazes on grasslands

This is North America's most common goose. It varies a lot in size and is easy to spot with its black head and neck broken up by a white band under its chin. It is a noisy bird and honks loudly, particularly when it is flying. Look for the large, dark wings and the white stripes on the chin and rump. It nests in the north, even on ponds in city parks. The female lays 4 to 6 white eggs. In the fall, look for flocks flying in a V-shape as they migrate south.

Black-crowned Night-Heron
(Nycticorax nycticorax)

As you can tell by its name, this heron has a black crown and eats mainly at night. It usually spends the day roosting motionless in a tree. It has a black back, gray wings, and white underparts. It hunches its short neck up so you can't see it. It nests in marshes and wetlands in much of the United States and southern Canada but moves south in the winter. It builds a substantial nest of sticks high up in a tree. The female lays 3 to 7 pale green eggs.

Family group: Heron
Size: 25 in (64 cm)
May be found in loose groups
Eats fish, frogs, and crustaceans

Double-crested Cormorant
(Phalacrocorax auritus)

This large, black bird has a double crest, but its crest is very hard to see. Look for its long, sharp bill and orange face instead. It flies with its neck stretched out. It regularly comes to freshwater lakes as well as the seacoast. Look for it spreading its wings to dry them off after a long time fishing underwater. It nests high up a cliff or in a tree. The female then lays 2 to 7 green-blue eggs.

Family group: Cormorant
Size: 30–36 in (76–91 cm)—Usually singly or in small flocks
Dives for fish—Also found on seacoasts

Clapper Rail
(Rallus longirostris)

Family group: Rail
Size: 14–15 in (36–38 cm)
Solitary and secretive
Eats small aquatic animals

Rails have short tails and short, rounded wings. The clapper rail is large and pale. Its upper parts are gray-brown, and its underparts have bands of gray and white. It has a long, yellowish bill and pinkish legs. You are more likely to hear a rail than see it. The clapper rail has a loud, raucous KEK-KEK-KEK-KEK call, which it mainly uses at dawn and dusk. The female lays 5 to 12 cream-colored eggs, lightly spotted with red-brown. Both the male and the female incubate the eggs.

Green Heron
(Butorides virescens)

Although this bird is a heron, it has short legs and a short neck and looks more like a bittern. Look for the chestnut face, neck, and breast; and dark green back and wings. It has a black crest that it raises when it is alarmed. It likes the thick vegetation around marshes and lakes, so you are most likely to see it flying from one patch of cover to another. Its nest is a platform of twigs hidden in a bush. The female lays 3 to 7 greenish-blue eggs.

Family group: Heron
Size: 18–19 in (46–48 cm)
Usually found alone
Eats fish
Also found in other wetlands

Pied-billed Grebe

(Podilymbus podiceps)

This is one of the less colorful grebes. It is brown on top and white at the rear. In the summer, look for the black patch on its throat and the black band near the edge of its bill. In the winter, its throat and bill are both a whitish color. You aren't likely to see grebes in flight. The pied-billed grebe builds its nest on water. This is a floating mass of water plants in which the female lays 5 to 7 white eggs, with splashes of blue or green.

Family group: Grebe
Size: 12–14 in (30–36 cm)—Usually in pairs
Dives in open water for small fish and water beetles

American Wigeon

(Anas americana)

You are most likely to see this duck grazing in fields and marshes in large flocks. It also is called "baldpate" because of the male's white forehead. The female has a gray head and brownish body. When they are flying, look for the white patches on their wings. They breed in Alaska, Canada, and the Northern States of the United States. They nest in the grasses beside lakes and marshes and lay 8 to 11 cream-colored eggs. In the fall, they migrate across the United States to the coast and Southern States, where you can see thousands of birds flocked together.

Family group: Duck
Size: 17–20 in (43–51 cm)—Forms large flocks
Dabbles in water for food and grazes in fields
Also found on coasts in the winter

Wood Duck

(Aix sponsa)

This is one of the most beautiful ducks in the world. It gets its name because it lives in woods near ponds or rivers. The female is mottled brown and spotted gray underneath. Wood ducks have sharp claws and sometimes perch on branches or stumps of trees. They build their nests in a hollow or hole in a tree and lay 10 to 15 cream-colored eggs. After the ducklings hatch, they use their sharp claws to climb out of the nest. Some wood ducks migrate to the Gulf Coast for the winter.

Family group:
Duck
Size: 17–20 in
(43–51 cm)
Usually found in pairs
Feeds in woodland streams and ponds

American Coot

(Fulica americana)

This bird is black all over except for a splash of white and chestnut on its forehead, its white bill, and the white outer feathers of its undertail. It spends most of its time swimming, but you might also see it running over the water to escape from danger or to take off into the air. It likes the open water but builds its floating nests in the cover around the edge of the water. Its nest is a bulky cup of plants in which the female lays 9 to 10 buff-colored eggs spotted with brown.

Family group: Rail
Size: 15–16 in (38–41 cm)
Usually found in flocks
Dives for water plants

Family group: Duck
Size: 20–28 in (51–71 cm)
Usually in groups
Dabbles in the water
for plants, seeds,
and snails

Mallard   *(Anas platyrhynchos)*

This is a common and familiar duck. During breeding season, the male mallard is easy to recognize by its bottle-green head, yellow bill, and brown throat with a white ring around its neck. The female is mottled brown with a yellow bill. Look for the flash of blue on the wings, seen when it flies. Like other dabbling ducks, mallards often "up-end" when they feed, so that only their tails can be seen above the water. The nest is a hollow in the ground lined with down. The female lays 8 to 12 white eggs.

Common Loon
(Gavia immer)

This bird looks a lot like a duck but, in the summer, it is easy to recognize by its black head and bill and boldly checkered black-and-white back. In the winter this loon's back is barred with gray. It spends the winter on the west and east coasts but moves north to northern lakes to breed. Listen for its eerie cries. Usually only one pair nest on a lake, although larger lakes may have two or more pairs. Its nest is a mass of vegetation near the edge of the water. The female lays 2 olive-green eggs with brown spots.

Family group: Loon
Size: 27–32 in (69–81 cm)—Usually in pairs
Dives for fish
Also found on coasts in winter

Common Merganser
(Mergus merganser)

This thin duck has a long thin bill with a serrated edge like a saw, which it uses to catch food. The male is black on top and white underneath with a bottle-green head. Look for the rounded crest at the back of his head. The female has a reddish head and gray body. In the winter you might see them in most of the United States. In the spring they fly north to breed in northern Canada and in the northeastern United States. They nest in holes in trees, among rocks, or undercut banks. The female lays 8 to 11 cream-colored eggs.

Family group: Duck
Size: 25 in (64 cm)—Usually in groups
Dives for fish and water creatures

Bald Eagle

Osprey

(Haliaeetus leucocephalus)
This magnificent bird is easy to recognize by its white head and neck, large yellow bill, and white tail, but it can only be seen in remote areas. It is the national bird of the United States and nearly became extinct because of shooting and pesticides. Their numbers have recently increased, but you can only see large flocks of these birds on the coasts of Alaska and British Columbia. It makes its nest of sticks at the top of a large tree, and the female lays 1 to 3 white eggs.
Family group: Hawk
Size: 31–37 in (79–94 cm)—Usually hunts alone
Eats fish—Also seen on sea coasts

(Pandion haliaetus)
This lightly built bird of prey is gray-brown on top and white underneath. Its wings are long and very narrow. When it flies, it arches them like a gull. Look for the patch of black at the bend of the wing. Watch it dive headlong toward the water, then plunge feet-first to pluck a fish out of the water. It breeds in much of North America and moves south to the southern coast for the winter. Its nest is a huge mound of twigs built on top of a tree. The female lays 2 to 4 creamy-colored eggs heavily spotted with brown.
Family group: Hawk—Size 21–25 in (53–64 cm)
Hunts alone—Eats fish

Belted Kingfisher
(Ceryle alcyon)

The female kingfisher has both a chestnut and a blue-gray band around her breast. The male has one blue-gray breast band only. This kingfisher is common in most of North America. Listen for its loud rattle. Look for it hovering over a pond, river, or stream before diving in headfirst for fish. Both male and female kingfishers use their heavy bills and strong feet to dig a long nest tunnel into a steep bank of earth, often on the side of a river or stream. The female then lays 5 to 7 white eggs.

Family group: Kingfisher
Size: 11–14 in (28–36 cm)
Usually on its own or in pairs
Dives for fish

Tree Swallow

(Tachycineta bicolor)
Swallows have slender bodies with long, pointed wings. The tree swallow is metallic blue on top and white underneath. You are most likely to see them in the air, flapping their wings and then gliding—twisting and turning to catch insects. Look for them in open areas near water. They build their nests in holes in trees, which they line with grass and feathers. The females lay 4 to 7 white eggs. In the fall thousands of birds flock together to migrate south.
Family group: Swallow—Size 5–6 in (13–15 cm)
Usually seen in flocks—Eats flying insects and some berries

Red-winged Blackbird

(Agelaius phoeniceus)
The male is glossy black with red patches bordered with buff-yellow on its wings. The female is streaked black and white on top and underneath and may have a suggestion of red on her wings. In early spring look for the males displaying their red patches near the marshes, trying to attack a mate. Listen for its KONK-LA-REE call. The female builds a nest in the dense growth around the marsh. Then she lays 3 to 6 blue-green eggs with dark spots.

Family group: Blackbird
Size: 8–9 in (20–23 cm)
Forms huge flocks in the winter
Eats seeds and insects
Also found on other kinds of wetlands

Spotted Sandpiper

(Actitis macularia)

In the summer this bird is brown on top and white underneath with regular black spots. In the winter its underparts are white only. On the ground it bobs and teeters as it walks along. In the air it flies low with stiff, jerky wing-beats. Listen for its call—a series of high-pitched WEET-WEET notes. The spotted sandpiper nests almost everywhere in the United States and southern Canada. It makes its nest in a dip in the ground and lays 3 or 4 tan eggs spotted with brown. In the winter it migrates to Central and South America.
Family group: Sandpiper
Size: 7–8 in (18–20 cm)

Usually on its own
Feeds in mud or shoreline on tiny animals

Marsh Wren

(Cistothorus palustris)

Wrens have slender, slightly curved bills and short tails, which often stand straight up over their backs. The marsh wren is a rich, rusty-brown, with white streaks on its brownish-black back and a white stripe over its eyes. It usually stays quiet and hidden among the reeds but sometimes perches on a cattail to sing. Listen for its distinctive TEK-TUK-T-JEJE song. It builds a large nest with a side entrance usually 12 inches (30 centimeters) above the water and anchored to the tall reeds. The female lays 3 or 6 brownish eggs, spotted with dark brown. It migrates to Southern and Coastal States for the winter.
Family group: Wren
Size: 4–5 in (10–13 cm)
Feeds on small insects and their larvae
Secretive

Find Out More

Glossary

adaptation: change made by an organism to better fit new conditions

belly: underside of a bird, below its wings

bib: area of a bird's body under its beak

broadleaf tree: tree with broad, flat leaves that usually drop off in the fall

brood: group of young birds hatched at the same time in a nest and cared for together

call: short sounds that a bird makes—perhaps to attract other birds to food or to warn about dangers

cap: area around the top of a bird's head; the cap is larger than the crown

cheek: area of a bird's head just below its eye

conifer: large group of trees or shrubs that bears its seeds in cones

crest: small tuft of feathers at the top of the head of some birds

crown: area at the very top of a bird's head; smaller than the cap

evergreen: tree or shrub, with needlelike or flat leaves, that keeps its leaves throughout the year

fertile: refers to land that is rich in nutrients and other things that help plants grow

fledgling: young bird just able to fly

forage: to hunt or search for food

homing: ability of a bird or other animal to return home from a great distance

incubation: sitting on eggs and keeping them warm in order to hatch them

mask: band of color that runs across a bird's eyes

mesquite: semidesert areas in the southwestern United States where thorny mesquite trees grow

migration: journey from one part of the world to another, usually made in both spring and fall

owl pellets: waste matter, usually containing animal bones, that an owl coughs up after it has eaten

plumage: feathers of a bird

roost: for a bird, the act of sleeping or a place to sleep

rump: area of a bird's body below the tail

savanna: grassland that has a few trees and bushes and limited rainfall

scrub: large area of thicket with stunted trees, shrubs, and bushes growing thickly together

secondary growth: plant growth in semi-open country with scattered trees and thickets

song: long musical sounds that a bird makes, often to attract a mate and establish a territory

talon: claw of a bird of prey, such as an eagle or owl

thicket: thick growth of scrub, underbrush, and small trees

tundra: vast, treeless region in cold regions of the world and on mountains

wattle: fleshy, wrinkled piece of skin, often brightly colored, that hangs from the chin or throat of some birds

wetland: area such as a marsh or pond that contains water during much or all of the year

Organizations

The **American Birding Association** is the largest all-birding organization in North America, and it publishes a bimonthly magazine, *Birding,* along with a monthly newsletter, *Winging It.* Contact: American Birding Association, Box 6599, Colorado Springs, Colorado 80934; (719) 578-9703. http://www.americanbirding.org

In Canada, the **Canadian Nature Federation** is a good starting point for birding information. Contact: Canadian Nature Federation, Suite 606, 1 Nicholas Street, Ottawa, Ontario K1N 7B7; (800) 267-4088. http://www.cnf.ca

The world-famous **Cornell Lab of Ornithology** accepts associate members and allows them the chance to take part in a number of cooperative research ventures, including Project FeederWatch. Members also receive the lab's quarterly magazine, *Living Bird.* Contact: Cornell Lab of Ornithology, 159 Sapsucker Woods Road, Ithaca, New York 14850; (800) 843-2473. http://www.birds.cornell.edu

The **National Audubon Society** is associated with birds, but in recent years it has become more involved in general environmental issues. Contact: National Audubon Society, 700 Broadway, New York, New York 10003; (212) 979-3000. http://www.audubon.org

There are also affiliated and independent Audubon Societies in every state.

Index

A

Abert's towhee, 53
acorn woodpecker, 29
American coot, 74
American crow, 14
American golden-plover, 54
American goldfinch, 46
American kestrel, 43
American redstart, 35
American robin, 8, 16
American wigeon, 70, 74
Arctic tern, 54

B

bald eagle, 76
baldpate. *See* American wigeon
Baltimore oriole, 10
barn owl, 10
barn swallow, 13, 54
barred owl, 27
beak, 7
belted kingfisher, 76
Bewick's wren, 32
bill, 7
bird
    development of, 4
    endangered, helping, 64–65
    feeding, 22–23, 38–39
    identifying, 6–7
    information sources, 78
    migration of, 54–55
birdbanding, 65
bird sanctuary, 64
bird-watching
    code for, 2
    feeding station for, 38–39
    guidelines for, 5, 48–49
black-and-white warbler, 37
black-billed cuckoo, 27
black-billed magpie, 45
blackbird, 77
black-capped chickadee, 20
black-crowned night-heron, 73
black-headed grosbeak, 34
black-throated sparrow, 50, 53

blind, for bird-watching, 48
bluebird, 40, 47
blue jay, 11
bobolink, 46
bobwhite, 43
broad-winged hawk, 30
brown creeper, 32
brown pelican, 68
bunting, 19

C

cactus wren, 53
Canada goose, 72
cardinal, 17
Carolina chickadee, 21
catbird, 15
cedar waxwing, 11
chat, 18
chickadee, 20, 21, 38
chihuahuan raven, 51
chimney swift, 8, 12
chipping sparrow, 16
city, birds in, 8–21
clapper rail, 73
coconut, as bird feed, 22
common grackle, 14
common loon, 75

common merganser, 70, 75
common nighthawk, 43
common tern, 66, 67
common yellowthroat, 18
coniferous forest, 56
Cooper's hawk, 30
coot, 74
cormorant, 73
Costa's hummingbird, 52
crane, 71
creeper, 32
crossbill, 56, 58, 59
crow, 14, 51
cuckoo, 27

D

dabbling duck, 70
dark-eyed junco, 21
desert, birds of, 50–53
dickcissel, 45
double-crested cormorant, 73
dove, 19, 52
downy woodpecker, 13
duck, 7, 66, 70, 74, 75

E

eagle, 7, 76
eastern bluebird, 47
eastern kingbird, 46
eastern meadowlark, 47
eastern phoebe, 21
eastern screech owl, 10
eastern towhee, 34
eastern wood-pewee, 32
egg, bird's, 4
egret, 71
elf owl, 51
endangered species, 64
European starling, 15
evening grosbeak, 61

F

falcon, 43
feeding, 22–23, 38–39
feet, of bird, 7
feral pigeon, 19
field sparrow, 44
finch, 7, 17, 24, 38, 46, 56
    see also grosbeak; pine siskin
first aid, for birds, 64
fledgling, 4
flicker, 12
flycatcher, 50, 53
footprint, bird, 49
forest, birds of
    broadleaf forests, 24–37
    evergreen forests, 56–63
fox sparrow, 32

G

garden, bird-friendly, 65
golden-crowned kinglet, 63
golden-plover, 54
goldfinch, 46
goose, 66, 72
grackle, 14
grassland, birds of, 40–47
gray catbird, 15
great blue heron, 72
great egret, 71
greater roadrunner, 51
greater yellowlegs, 71
great horned owl, 27

Additional Resources

Backyard Birds Roger Tory Peterson, editor (Houghton Mifflin, 1996).

Backyard Birds of Summer Carol Lerner (Morrow, 1996) and ***Backyard Birds of Winter*** (1994).

Birds in Your Backyard Barbara Herkert (Dawn Publications, 2001).

Birds of North America Noel Grove (Hugh Lauter Levin, 1996).

Lives of North American Birds Kenn Kaufman (Houghton Mifflin, 1996) and ***Birds of North America*** (2000).

National Audubon Society First Field Guide: Birds Scott Weidensaul (Scholastic, 1998).

The Sibley Guide to Birds David Allen Sibley (Knopf, 2000) and ***Birding Basics*** (2002).

Index

grebe, 74
green heron, 73
grosbeak, 34, 35, 56, 58, 61
grouse, 26, 62
gull, 7, 54, 66, 67

H

hairy woodpecker, 29
harrier, 42
hawk, 7, 54, 66
  forest, 24, 30, 31
  grassland and savanna, 40, 42
hermit thrush, 60
heron, 7, 70–73
herring gull, 66, 67
hooded warbler, 36
horned lark, 40, 47
house finch, 17
house sparrow, 16
house wren, 13
hummingbird, 11, 52, 54

I

Inca dove, 52
indigo bunting, 19

J

jay, 11
junco, 21

K

kestrel, 40, 43
killdeer, 40, 44
kingbird, 40, 46
kingfisher, 76
kinglet, 63

L

lake, birds of, 70–77
lark, 40, 47
laughing gull, 67
lazuli bunting, 19
legs, of bird, 7
lesser yellowlegs, 71
loggerhead shrike, 42
loon, 68, 75

M

magnolia warbler, 60
magpie, 40, 45
mallard, 75
marsh, birds of
  freshwater, 70–77
  seashores, 66–69
marsh wren, 77
martin, 12
meadowlark, 40, 47
merganser, 70, 75
migration, bird, 54–55
mockingbird, 15
mourning dove, 19

N

Nashville warbler, 36
nighthawk, 43
night-heron, 73
nightjar, 43
northern bobwhite, 43
northern cardinal, 17
northern flicker, 12
northern harrier, 42
northern mockingbird, 15
northern shrike, 42
notebook, field, 49
nuthatch, 63

O

oil, bird covered by, 64
orchard oriole, 34
oriole, 10, 34
osprey, 76
ovenbird, 33
owl, 10, 27, 51, 62

P

park, birds in, 8–21
peanut, as bird feed, 22
pelican, 68
pewee. See wood-pewee
pheasant, 7, 45
phoebe, 21
pied-billed grebe, 74
pigeon, 19, 38, 52
pileated woodpecker, 28
pine grosbeak, 58
pine siskin, 59
pine warbler, 59

plain titmouse, 20
plaster cast of footprints, 49
plover, 54, 69
pollution, 64
prairie warbler, 36
projects
  bird warning, 55
  bird-watching expedition, 48–49
  feeding birds, 22–23, 38–39
  helping birds, 64–65
purple martin, 12

Q

quail, 52

R

rail, 73
raven, 51
red-breasted nuthatch, 63
red crossbill, 58
red-eyed vireo, 37
redheaded woodpecker, 28
red-shouldered hawk, 31
redstart, 35
red-tailed hawk, 40, 42
red-throated loon, 68
red-winged blackbird, 77
ricebird. See bobolink
ring-billed gull, 67
ring-necked pheasant, 45
river, birds of, 70–77
roadrunner, 51
robin, 8, 16
rock dove, 19
rose-breasted grosbeak, 35
ruby-crowned kinglet, 63
ruby-throated hummingbird, 11, 54
ruddy turnstone, 69
ruffed grouse, 26
rufous hummingbird, 11

S

salt marsh, birds of, 66
sanderling, 69
sandpiper, 7, 68, 69, 77

sapsucker, 29
savanna, birds of, 40–47
scaled quail, 52
scarlet tanager, 35
scientific names, 2
screech owl, 10
seashore, birds of the, 66–69
seed, as bird feed, 22
semipalmated plover, 69
sharp-shinned hawk, 30
shrike, 42
siskin, 59
sketching birds, 5, 49
snowy egret, 71
song sparrow, 17
sparrow, 54
  city park and suburb, 16, 17
  desert, 50, 53
  forest, 24, 32
  grassland and savanna, 44
spotted owl, 62
spotted sandpiper, 77
spruce grouse, 62
starling, 15, 38
suburb, birds in, 8–21
suet cake, 23
swallow, 12, 13, 54, 66, 77
swan, 72
swift, 7, 8, 12

T

tanager, 35, 60
tern, 54, 66, 67
thrush, 24, 33, 56, 60, 66
titmouse, 20
towhee, 34, 53
tree swallow, 77
tufted titmouse, 20
tundra swan, 72
turkey, 26
turkey vulture, 31
turnstone, 69
tyrant flycatcher, 21

V

veery, 33
vermilion flycatcher, 50, 53

vesper sparrow, 44
vireo, 37
vulture, 31

W

warbler
  city park and suburb, 18
  desert, 54
  forest, 24, 36, 37, 56,
    59–61
  seashore and marsh, 66

waxwing, 11
western bluebird, 47
western kingbird, 46
western meadowlark, 47
western screech owl, 10
western tanager, 60
western wood-pewee, 32
whippoorwill, 31
white-eyed vireo, 37
white-throated sparrow, 17
white-winged crossbill, 59

wigeon, 70, 74
wild turkey, 26
willet, 68
Wilson's warbler, 36
wing shapes, 7
wood duck, 74
woodland hawk, 24
woodpecker, 7, 12, 13,
  24, 28, 29
wood-pewee, 32
wood thrush, 33

wren, 13, 32, 53, 77

Y

yellow-bellied sapsucker,
  29
yellow-billed cuckoo, 27
yellow-breasted chat, 18
yellowlegs, 71
yellow-rumped warbler, 61
yellowthroat, 18
yellow warbler, 18

See *World Book's Science & Nature Guides Resources & Cumulative Index* volume for an explanation of the system used by scientists to classify living things.